Collins

Key Stage 3

World Religions: Hinduism, Buddhism and Sikhism

Tristan Elby and Neil McKain

Series Editor: Robert Orme

William Collins' dream of knowledge for all began with the publication of his first book in 1819. A self-educated mill worker, he not only enriched millions of lives, but also founded a flourishing publishing house. Today, staying true to this spirit, Collins books are packed with inspiration, innovation and practical expertise. They place you at the centre of a world of possibility and give you exactly what you need to explore it.

Collins. Freedom to teach

Published by Collins
An imprint of HarperCollins*Publishers*
The News Building
1 London Bridge Street
London SE1 9GF

HarperCollins*Publishers*
Macken House
39/40 Mayor Street Upper
Dublin 1
DO1 C9W8
Ireland

10

ISBN 978-0-00-822769-2

Publisher: Joanna Ramsay
Editor: Hannah Dove
Authors: Tristan Elby and Neil McKain
Series Editor: Robert Orme
Development Editor: Sonya Newland
Project Manager: Emily Hooton
Copy-editor: Jill Morris
Image researcher: Shelley Noronha
Proof-readers: Ros and Chris Davies
Cover designer: We Are Laura
Cover images: robert stoetzel/Alamy; Chonlatip
Hirunsatitporn/Shutterstock; saiko3p/Shutterstock
Production controller: Rachel Weaver
Typesetter: QBS
Printed and bound by Ashford Colour Press Ltd

Contents

Introduction

It is not easy to define what makes something a religion. In some religions one god is worshipped, in others many gods are worshipped, and in some no god is worshipped at all. Some religions have a single founder. In others, there is not one person who starts it or one clear moment when it began. To make things more complicated, there are often strong differences of opinion between and even within particular religions. Two people following the same religion can believe opposing things and follow their religion in strikingly different ways. Within any religion, some people build their whole lives around their beliefs while others are less committed to their religion but still think of themselves as part of it. Followers of all religions believe that they have found truth, but their ideas about what is true differ greatly.

Approximately 84 per cent of people in the world today follow a religion and experts predict that this will rise to 87 per cent by 2050. The most followed religion in the UK is Christianity, but there are also followers of many other religions including Islam, Judaism, Buddhism, Hinduism and Sikhism. In recent times there has also been a big increase in the number of people in the UK who do not follow any religion. Some are atheists which means that they do not believe there is a god or gods. Others are agnostics meaning they are not sure if a god or gods exist. Others might believe there is a god or gods, but choose not to belong to a religion.

By studying the beliefs and ways of life of millions of people around the world, you will gain a greater understanding of the past, the modern world and humanity itself. You will explore questions that have troubled humankind through the ages and examine the diverse ways in which these questions have been answered. In a world where religion has and continues to play such a large role, the importance of understanding it is as great as ever.

Robert Orme (Series Editor)

Concise topic introductions set the scene and focus your learning.

Engaging photos illustrate the key ideas.

End-of-topic questions are designed to check and consolidate your understanding.

Fact boxes provide bite-sized details.

Key fact boxes help you to revise and remember the main points from each unit.

Key vocabulary lists for each unit help you define and remember important terms.

Key people boxes summarise the key figures from the unit.

Knowledge organisers can be used to revise and quiz yourself on key dates, definitions and descriptions.

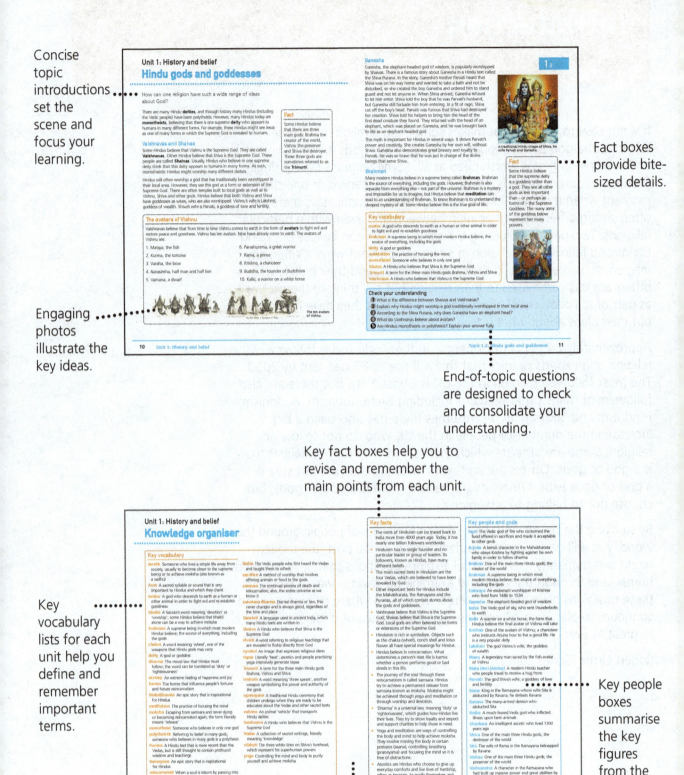

Hinduism

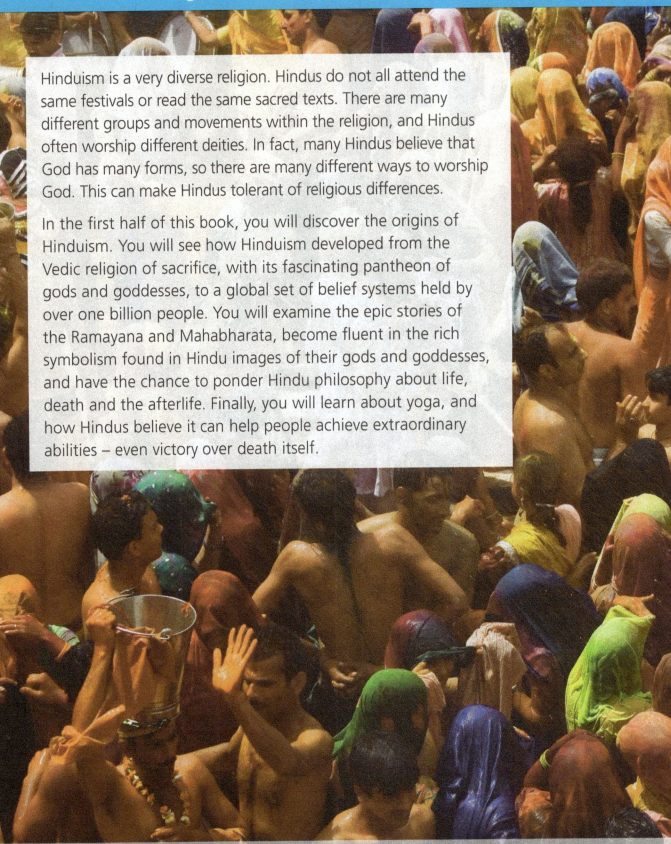

History and belief

Hinduism is a very diverse religion. Hindus do not all attend the same festivals or read the same sacred texts. There are many different groups and movements within the religion, and Hindus often worship different deities. In fact, many Hindus believe that God has many forms, so there are many different ways to worship God. This can make Hindus tolerant of religious differences.

In the first half of this book, you will discover the origins of Hinduism. You will see how Hinduism developed from the Vedic religion of sacrifice, with its fascinating pantheon of gods and goddesses, to a global set of belief systems held by over one billion people. You will examine the epic stories of the Ramayana and Mahabharata, become fluent in the rich symbolism found in Hindu images of their gods and goddesses, and have the chance to ponder Hindu philosophy about life, death and the afterlife. Finally, you will learn about yoga, and how Hindus believe it can help people achieve extraordinary abilities – even victory over death itself.

What is Hinduism?

The ancient religion of Hinduism has over one billion followers today, but do all Hindus share the same beliefs?

Various aspects of the religion that we call Hinduism can be traced to India over 3000 years ago. This makes it one of the oldest religions in the world, and the oldest of the six major world religions. Today, Hinduism is the third-largest religion in the world, with over a billion followers worldwide, known as Hindus. The word 'Hindu' comes from a river called the Indus that flowed through the area of northwest India where Hinduism developed. Most Hindus still live in India, but the religion has also spread to other countries. There are more than 800,000 Hindus living in Britain.

The Indus river in Ladakh, India.

A diverse religion

Unlike many other religions, there was not one person who founded Hinduism, nor was there one specific moment when it began. There is no single powerful leader or group of leaders in Hinduism. Hindus have many different beliefs and they do not all worship the same gods and goddesses. Some people have even described Hinduism as a collection of many different religions rather than one religion.

There is no one book that tells Hindus what to believe or how to live; there are many different books that Hindus can choose to read, or not. However, Hindus view the four **Vedas** as sacred. These are the oldest Hindu texts and, like many other Hindu books, they are written in **Sanskrit**. The Vedas tell us what Hindus believed and how they worshipped 3000 years ago.

What was Vedic Hinduism like?

The Vedas mention a large number of gods and goddesses, and the Vedic people were **polytheistic**. Many of the Vedic gods were in charge of parts of the natural world that were useful or potentially dangerous to the Vedic people. For example, Rudra was a much-feared god who inflicted illness upon farm animals if he was unhappy with the way people were worshipping him. Indra was the god of sky, who sent thunderbolts to earth. People also worshipped gods of the sun, earth, fire and dawn.

Fact

The first of the four Vedas, the Rig Veda, says 'Let noble thoughts come to us from all directions.' This shows that Hindus should welcome good ideas wherever they come from and that they are comfortable with diversity. One Hindu hymn compares different religions or paths to God with hundreds of different streams and rivers, which ultimately end up in the same ocean. Many Hindus today believe that other religious beliefs may be equally true, and they do not try to convert others to Hinduism.

These Vedic gods were deeply relevant to life in ancient India, where a bad harvest or the premature death of animals could spell disaster for people who depended on these things. As Hinduism spread and society developed, Hindus began to change the gods and goddesses they worshipped. However, most Vedic deities still have a place in Hindu symbolism and worship today.

Indra, the king of the Vedic gods, riding his three-headed elephant. In his hand is an object that represents his weapon – a thunderbolt.

Animal sacrifice

One way in which the Vedic people tried to keep their gods happy was through the **sacrifice** of food and animals. The Vedas refer to sacrifices of goats, oxen and even horses. This would have been done on a special sacrificial altar sometimes in the shape

A Vedic fire altar. These are still used for sacrifices in some parts of the world.

of a falcon or eagle. Agni (the god of fire, also the Sanskrit word for fire) consumed the food offered in the sacrifice. This made it acceptable to the gods.

Vedic Hindus believed that gods and humans helped each other. Humans offered the gods food and animals in order to please them, and in return they believed that the gods would send good weather, fine crops and keep their animals healthy. For this reason, Agni was a very important god, because the sacrifices he made possible caused the gods to rain blessings down on earth.

Over time, animal sacrifice gradually became a lot less popular, but it does still exist among Hindus in some parts of the world.

How did Hinduism develop?

One reason why Hinduism is so diverse today is because it developed among many different people over a long period of time and across a very large area. Different people had different ideas in different places at different times. The Hinduism that exists today is the result of a long process of change and development over 3000 years. In the following pages, you will learn more about this journey.

Key vocabulary

polytheistic Referring to belief in many gods; someone who believes in many gods is a polytheist

sacrifice A method of worship that involves offering animals or food to the gods

Sanskrit A language used in ancient India, which many Hindu texts are written in

Vedas A collection of sacred writings, literally meaning 'knowledge'

Check your understanding

1. When and where did Hinduism begin?
2. What are Hindu sacred texts called and in what language were they written?
3. Explain at least two differences between Vedic religion and modern Hinduism.
4. Why is there so much diversity in Hinduism today?
5. How is Hinduism different from one other religion that you have studied?

Unit 1: History and belief
Hindu gods and goddesses

How can one religion have such a wide range of ideas about God?

There are many Hindu **deities**, and through history many Hindus (including the Vedic people) have been polytheists. However, many Hindus today are **monotheists**, believing that there is one supreme **deity** who appears to humans in many different forms. For example, these Hindus might see Jesus as one of many forms in which the Supreme God is revealed to humans.

Vaishnavas and Shaivas

Some Hindus believe that Vishnu is the Supreme God. They are called **Vaishnavas**. Other Hindus believe that Shiva is the Supreme God. These people are called **Shaivas**. Usually, Hindus who believe in one supreme deity think that this deity appears to humans in many forms. As such, monotheistic Hindus might worship many different deities.

Hindus will often worship a god that has traditionally been worshipped in their local area. However, they see this god as a form or extension of the Supreme God. There are often temples built to local gods as well as to Vishnu, Shiva and other gods. Hindus believe that both Vishnu and Shiva have goddesses as wives, who are also worshipped. Vishnu's wife is Lakshmi, goddess of wealth. Shiva's wife is Parvati, a goddess of love and fertility.

> ### Fact
>
> Some Hindus believe that there are three main gods: Brahma the creator of the world, Vishnu the preserver and Shiva the destroyer. These three gods are sometimes referred to as the **Trimurti**.

The avatars of Vishnu

Vaishnavas believe that from time to time Vishnu comes to earth in the form of **avatars** to fight evil and restore peace and goodness. Vishnu has ten avatars. Nine have already come to earth. The avatars of Vishnu are:

1. Matsya, the fish
2. Kurma, the tortoise
3. Varaha, the boar
4. Narasimha, half man and half lion
5. Vamana, a dwarf

6. Parashurama, a great warrior
7. Rama, a prince
8. Krishna, a charioteer
9. Buddha, the founder of Buddhism
10. Kalki, a warrior on a white horse

The ten avatars of Vishnu.

Ganesha

Ganesha, the elephant-headed god of wisdom, is popularly worshipped by Shaivas. There is a famous story about Ganesha in a Hindu text called the Shiva Purana. In the story, Ganesha's mother Parvati heard that Shiva was on his way home and wanted to take a bath and not be disturbed, so she created the boy Ganesha and ordered him to stand guard and not let anyone in. When Shiva arrived, Ganesha refused to let him enter. Shiva told the boy that he was Parvati's husband, but Ganesha still forbade him from entering. In a fit of rage, Shiva cut off the boy's head. Parvati was furious that Shiva had destroyed her creation. Shiva told his helpers to bring him the head of the first dead creature they found. They returned with the head of an elephant, which was placed on Ganesha, and he was brought back to life as an elephant-headed god.

This myth is important for Hindus in several ways. It shows Parvati's power and creativity. She creates Ganesha by her own will, without Shiva. Ganesha also demonstrates great bravery and loyalty to Parvati. He was so brave that he was put in charge of the divine beings that serve Shiva.

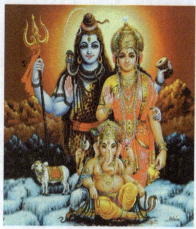

A traditional Hindu image of Shiva, his wife Parvati and Ganesha.

Brahman

Many modern Hindus believe in a supreme being called **Brahman**. Brahman is the source of everything, including the gods. However, Brahman is also separate from everything else – not part of the universe. Brahman is a mystery and impossible for us to imagine, but Hindus believe that **meditation** can lead to an understanding of Brahman. To know Brahman is to understand the deepest mystery of all. Some Hindus believe this is the true goal of life.

Key vocabulary

avatar A god who descends to earth as a human or other animal in order to fight evil and re-establish goodness

Brahman A supreme being in which most modern Hindus believe; the source of everything, including the gods

deity A god or goddess

meditation The practice of focusing the mind

monotheist Someone who believes in only one god

Shaiva A Hindu who believes that Shiva is the Supreme God

Trimurti A term for the three main Hindu gods Brahma, Vishnu and Shiva

Vaishnava A Hindu who believes that Vishnu is the Supreme God

Fact

Some Hindus believe that the supreme deity is a goddess rather than a god. They see all other gods as less important than – or perhaps as forms of – the Supreme Goddess. The many arms of the goddess below represent her many powers.

Check your understanding

1 What is the difference between Shaivas and Vaishnavas?

2 Explain why Hindus might worship a god traditionally worshipped in their local area.

3 According to the Shiva Purana, why does Ganesha have an elephant head?

4 What do Vaishnavas believe about avatars?

5 Are Hindus monotheists or polytheists? Explain your answer fully.

Unit 1: History and belief
How do Hindus use symbols?

What are the secrets of Hindu symbols?

Vishnu

Hindu deities are often shown as having several arms. This is to symbolise that gods and goddesses have superior powers to humans. In the picture below, Vishnu has four arms. This may represent the four directions of the compass, showing that Vishnu is the supreme ruler of the universe who rules in all directions. Vishnu is also holding a different object in each of his hands. These objects are all Hindu **symbols**.

The round object is a **chakra** ('wheel'), which is a hugely powerful divine weapon. When someone throws a chakra, it returns, so it symbolises Vishnu's power, which cannot be exhausted.

In this hand, Vishnu holds a conch shell. Conches produce a distinctive sound when blown, so this could represent both the breath of life that the god breathes into living things and the sacred sound **Aum** (or Om) that Hindus chant.

The flower Vishnu holds is a lotus, which can represent purity. It can also symbolise Lakshmi, his wife, who gives him his energy. Some Hindus see the lotus flower as representing detachment, which means not getting too attached to the pleasures or opportunities life brings.

In this hand, Vishnu holds a powerful, heavy weapon called a mace. This symbolises the way that Vishnu sometimes takes a physical form (avatar) in order to fight evil.

Shiva

The picture of Shiva is a good example of a single image containing a great deal of symbolism. Shiva has his legs crossed, as if meditating. Shiva is highly praised for his ability to sit absorbed in perfect meditation. Hindus often meditate in simple, remote locations, and here Shiva is sitting on Mount Kailash, a sacred and legendary mountain where many Hindus believe he and his wife Parvati live. The god is wearing a simple animal skin, just as someone who has dedicated himself to meditation would.

Hindus believe that meditation can bring great powers. The three white lines on Shiva's forehead are called the **vibhuti**. This symbol represents his superhuman powers and the fact that he is everywhere in the universe. At the centre of Shiva's forehead is his 'third eye'. This represents the wisdom that Shiva has gained through meditation.

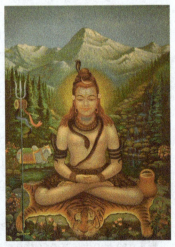

Shiva sitting in meditation.

The bull standing behind Shiva is called Nandi. Hindu deities usually have what is known as a **vahana**, a vehicle, so that they can travel around, and a deity's vahana will usually appear alongside him or her in images. Bulls are strong and dedicated, just as Shiva is strong and dedicated to doing good. However, bulls are also independent and headstrong, so the bull can also suggest that Shiva is a slightly wild, untamed god. Nandi the bull can also represent a devoted follower of Shiva.

Vishnu has a mace as a weapon, whereas Shiva has a trident, called a **trishula**. Some Hindus believe that, at the end of time, Shiva will destroy the universe with this weapon so that it can be created again.

Snake symbols

If you look closely at the images on these pages, you can see a snake in the ocean underneath Vishnu and another around Shiva's neck. The snake near Vishnu could be a symbol of infinity – a snake that is infinitely long, just as Vishnu is infinitely powerful. It could also refer to a Hindu myth about Vasuki, the king of serpents. In this myth, the gods use Vasuki to churn the ocean in order to extract a liquid that would grant immortality. The churning also produces a poison, which Shiva drinks from the mouth of Vasuki in order to save others, so the snake around his neck could represent this.

Activity

Draw and label four symbols often found in pictures of Vishnu and Shiva.

Key vocabulary

Aum A sacred syllable or sound that is very important to Hindus and which they chant

chakra A word meaning 'wheel', one of the weapons that Hindu gods may carry

symbol An image that expresses religious ideas

trishula A word meaning 'three spears', another weapon symbolising the power and authority of the gods

vahana An animal 'vehicle' that transports Hindu deities

vibhuti The three white lines on Shiva's forehead, which represent his superhuman powers

Sculpture of Shiva sitting in meditation on Ganges river in Rishikesh, India, 2011.

Check your understanding

1 What is a symbol?

2 What could Vishnu's four arms represent?

3 Explain which symbols in the picture of Shiva refer to meditation.

4 Explain what the weapons of Shiva and Vishnu might symbolise for Hindus.

5 Explain, with examples, why symbols are important in Hinduism.

Unit 1: History and belief
Sacred texts

Where did Hindu texts come from and what is in them?

The Vedas

Nearly all Hindus agree that the four Vedas are sacred and revealed by God. The Vedas contain hymns to Hindu gods and goddesses as well as teachings about the soul and the afterlife, and detailed instructions on how to worship and perform rituals.

The Vedas are sometimes called **shruti**, which literally means 'heard', because this is how Hindus believe the Vedas were first received. The Vedic people who received the Vedas were called **Rishis**. They were great meditators and this allowed them to see and hear things that ordinary humans could not. After the Rishis 'heard' the Vedas, they taught them to priests, who memorised and recited them to the next generation. This continued for many centuries. Hindus believe that the Vedas were passed on so accurately that they are almost like a recording of what people were reciting 3000 years ago.

The Mahabharata and the Ramayana

There are other holy or sacred texts in Hinduism. Among the oldest are two epic stories known as the **Mahabharata** and the **Ramayana**. Each of these is a very long story made up of many shorter stories.

The Ramayana is about a warrior called King Rama and his beautiful wife Sita. The story tells of how a terrifying demon king called Ravana kidnapped Sita because he wanted her to be his wife. In his search for Sita, Rama came across Hanuman, king of the monkeys, who agreed to help him. A message was passed to all the monkeys in the world to find Sita. The monkeys passed the message on to the bears, who were led by their king, Jambavan. Eventually, Hanuman found Sita imprisoned on the island of Lanka. A wise monkey called Nala assisted Hanuman by building a huge bridge to Lanka. In the battle to rescue Sita, Rama killed Ravana with a magic arrow. As Rama and Sita returned home to the city of Ayodhya, people lit lights to guide them and welcome them back.

The Ramayana is inspiring for Hindus because it gives examples of good Hindu behaviour. Hanuman shows great loyalty to Rama by helping him, while Sita is a brave, loyal wife who does not give up hope that Rama will rescue her. The story also has an inspirational message that good defeats evil.

Fact

Many scholars of Hinduism believe that the process of composing the Vedas began around 1500 BCE, and it probably took almost a thousand years for all four Vedas to be composed.

Part of the Rig Veda written in Sanskrit.

Sita being abducted by the many-armed demon Ravana.

The Mahabharata is a tale of a devastating war between two sides of the same family. It contains so many smaller stories that it spans several volumes and is more than twice as long as the Christian Bible. Most Hindus do not read all of the Mahabharata, but many find a small part of it called the Bhagavad Gita ('The Song of the Lord') particularly inspiring. In the Bhagavadgita, a conversation takes place on a battlefield between a warrior called Arjuna and his charioteer, Krishna, an avatar of Vishnu. At first, Arjuna does not realise that Krishna is an avatar. As they talk, Krishna tells Arjuna how to live a good life, how people should live together in society and what happens after death. Krishna then reveals his true form to Arjuna. Arjuna is overwhelmed that he has seen and talked to God.

The Puranas

Even after the Vedas were complete, many Hindus continued to compose sacred texts. These are known as the **Puranas**, which means 'ancient ones'. Hindus who worship Vishnu consider the Bhagavata Purana to be a very holy text. It teaches about the need to show Vishnu complete devotion. Other Puranas describe what the end of the current age will be like. They predict that the world will be very chaotic and there will be much evil. Some Vaishnavas believe that at this time Vishnu will take the form of Kalki, a warrior on a white horse holding a blazing sword. Kalki will fight a war against the forces of evil, which will end in a great battle against two demon generals. All evil will be destroyed, marking the start of a new golden age.

Different Hindu communities recite or celebrate different texts because they focus on different gods or goddesses.

Key vocabulary

Mahabharata An epic story that is inspirational for Hindus

Purana A Hindu text that is more recent than the Vedas, but is still thought to contain profound wisdom and teachings

Ramayana An epic story that is inspirational for Hindus

Rishis The Vedic people who first heard the Vedas and taught them to others

shruti A word referring to religious teachings that are revealed to Rishis directly from God

Check your understanding

1 Why are the Vedas sometimes called 'shruti'?

2 When were the Vedas written and how long did this process take?

3 Explain what happens in the Ramayana and why Hindus find it inspiring.

4 Explain what happens in the Bhagavad Gita and why Hindus find it inspiring.

5 What are the Puranas and what might they teach Hindus?

Unit 1: History and belief
Karma, samsara and moksha

How do Hindus believe that their next lives will be decided?

Samsara

Hindus believe that their current life is just one of many lives they have already led and will lead in the future. They believe that when a person dies his or her soul is reborn in a new body. This will not necessarily be a human body – the person's next life could be as an animal, an insect or a species completely unknown to us.

A person's next life depends on **karma**. Good deeds store up good karma and bad deeds store up bad karma. Depending on a person's actions, he or she might be **reincarnated** as any type of creature, or even find him or herself in heaven or hell. All these reincarnations are temporary.

Samsara is a Sanskrit word that Hindus use to describe the continual journey of the soul through many reincarnations. Samsara also refers to the universe within which these reincarnations take place. Hindus believe that we are all journeying through samsara, and have been for billions of years.

For Hindus, good deeds, such as this woman donating food, store up good karma.

Moksha

Hindus believe that people can have many positive experiences within samsara, and many fulfilling lives. However, there will also be a large number of painful and unpleasant lives, although people tend to forget each life as they move to the next one.

To break this cycle, Hindus want to achieve **moksha** – a permanent escape from samsara.

It is difficult to describe moksha. Because samsara is essentially the whole universe, moksha is completely unlike anything people have experienced in any of their lives. Generally, however, achieving moksha means you are not reborn and do not change any more. There is no further suffering of any kind. Many Hindus believe that moksha will involve everlasting bliss and inner peace. Some believe that moksha involves being united with God forever.

This mural in a palace in India shows the elephant king Gajendra achieving moksha.

Others think that moksha is when you realise that you were never different from God in the first place – all of samsara was just an illusion that made you think that you were separate from God.

Nirvana

Buddhists also believe in karma and samsara and try to achieve freedom from samsara. They call this achieving nirvana or parinirvana. However, Buddhists tend to disagree with Hindus about whether they will be united with God after escaping samsara. Many Buddhists think that nirvana is a state of perfect peace, which will not involve any gods or goddesses at all.

Achieving moksha

Achieving moksha can take many lifetimes. One way of achieving moksha is through yoga (see pages 22–23). People who are excellent at yoga, called yogins, are believed to be able to purify themselves of bad karma. If you meditate and develop your mind and body in the right way, you will eventually be freed from any further reincarnation. Yoga can involve fasting and long and painful exercises. It also requires meditation – focusing the mind completely on God.

Another way of achieving moksha is through **bhakti**, which is Sanskrit for 'devotion' or 'worship'. This involves becoming increasingly devoted to God throughout each of your lifetimes. As your worship and devotion increases, your soul will be purified. Eventually, like the yogins, you will achieve moksha.

This man is trying to achieve moksha through yoga and meditation.

The Upanishads are very old philosophical texts that explain some key Hindu ideas about life after death.

❝ And here is he born either as a grasshopper, or a fish, or a bird, or a lion, or a boar, or a serpent, or a tiger, or a man, or some other creature, according to his deeds and his knowledge. ❞
Kaushitaki Brahmana Upanishad

❝ When a caterpillar has come to the end of a blade of grass, it reaches out to another blade, and draws itself over to it. In the same way the soul, having coming to the end of one life, reaches out to another body, and draws itself over to it. ❞
Brihadaranyaka Upanishad

❝ As a man casts off his worn-out clothes, and takes other new ones in their place, so does the embodied soul cast off his worn-out bodies, and enter others anew. ❞
Bhagavad Gita

Key vocabulary

bhakti A Sanskrit word meaning 'devotion' or 'worship'; some Hindus believe that bhakti alone can be a way to achieve moksha

karma The forces that influence people's fortune and future reincarnations

moksha Escaping from samsara and never dying or becoming reincarnated again; the word literally means 'release'

reincarnated When a soul is reborn by passing into a new body

samsara The continual process of death and reincarnation; also, the entire universe as we know it

Activity

Draw and label three images that illustrate karma, samsara and moksha.

Check your understanding

1 Explain what Hindus mean by reincarnation.
2 How is a soul's next reincarnation decided?
3 What is moksha and why is it difficult to imagine what moksha is like?
4 Describe two ways to achieve moksha.
5 'Karma, reincarnation and moksha do not exist.' Discuss this statement.

Unit 1: History and belief
Dharma

How do people in different situations follow the same universal law of dharma?

In Hinduism, people's thoughts and behaviour store up karma, which affects their next lives. This is one reason why Hindus try to behave morally. When it comes to living a good life, the key idea in Hinduism is **dharma**, which can be broadly translated as 'duty', 'righteousness' or 'moral law'.

Hindus believe that the Supreme Being has revealed dharma to people through sacred texts and that to follow dharma successfully is to achieve their deepest purpose. Following dharma carefully is likely to create good karma and cause a good reincarnation in the next life.

How do you follow dharma?

Everyone follows dharma in different ways. For King Rama, following dharma meant ruling justly and setting a good example for his people. Rama was also a husband whose wife had been kidnapped. In that situation, dharma meant rescuing Sita no matter how dangerous it was. For Sita, dharma meant being loyal to Rama and not giving up hope that she would be rescued. These examples show that following dharma is not always easy.

For many Hindus today, being loyal and respectful to their families and communities would be behaving in accordance with dharma. Giving to charity and showing kindness to those less fortunate is also part of dharma. In the UK, many Hindus support Sewa UK, a Hindu charity that provides help in places of need and supports people with disabilities. This is a very dharmic activity.

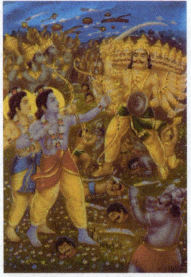
Rama, assisted by the monkey army of Hanuman, defeats the demon Ravana. He is upholding dharma by saving his wife and defeating evil, despite the danger.

A Sewa UK charity shop. Helping those in need is part of the Hindu duty of 'sewa' or 'service'.

Dharma in Hindu texts

Dharma is sometimes difficult to follow, and Hindu texts include many examples of people trying hard to follow dharma in difficult situations. In the Bhagavad Gita, Krishna tells Arjuna that he must fight in the war of the Mahabharata because it is righteous. Krishna says that no matter how difficult it might be – even if it means fighting family members – Arjuna must follow dharma by doing his duty as a warrior on the side of goodness and justice.

Stages of life

Hindus believe that ways of following dharma can change depending on your stage of life. For young people, dharma could mean studying hard and respecting their families. From a young age, many Hindu boys 'take the sacred thread'. This is a thin cord that they accept to show that they are ready to learn sacred scriptures like the Vedas. They receive it in a ceremony called the **upanayana**, and they wear the thread for the rest of their lives. Hindus believe that continuing this tradition preserves dharma and pleases God. In earlier times, the tradition was only for boys in the top three classes of society (see pages 36–37). Nowadays, it is more widespread, and girls sometimes receive a similar initiation.

Once Hindus reach adulthood, there are new important parts of dharma. These include marrying, raising children and taking care of their parents, especially when they are elderly.

Eternal dharma

Some Hindus believe in **sanatana dharma**. This means 'eternal' or 'timeless' dharma. The world has changed a lot over the course of history, but for Hindus some things remain the same. Whatever the time and place, showing devotion to God, being loyal to your family and community, and making the best possible use of your talents and situation are always part of dharma.

Hindus believe that God has made sure that the universe is fundamentally good and lawful. Evil and chaos may sometimes seem powerful, but dharma still exists and will eventually be restored. Vaishnavas believe that Vishnu has taken different forms in different times and places, but whether he is a fish, a dwarf or a prince, he still upholds the same eternal dharma.

A boy who has taken the sacred thread.

Key vocabulary

dharma The moral law that Hindus must follow; the word can be translated as 'duty' or 'righteousness'

sanatana dharma Eternal dharma or law; this never changes and is always good, regardless of the time and place

upanayana A traditional Hindu ceremony that children undergo when they are ready to be educated about the Vedas and other sacred texts

Check your understanding

1. What does the word 'dharma' mean?
2. What did behaving in accordance with dharma mean for Sita?
3. Describe the two ways that Rama needed to follow dharma in the Ramayana.
4. Explain how dharma changes at different stages of life.
5. Using these pages and page 12, describe how Vishnu upholds dharma.

Unit 1: History and belief
What is yoga?

Can yoga help people escape the cycle of samsara?

What is yoga?

Today, many non-Hindus practise **yoga**, but it has been part of Hinduism for thousands of years. Yoga is a Sanskrit word meaning 'yoke', a harness that is placed on an animal to control it. Through yoga, Hindus try to yoke, or control, their mind and body. Yoga can also mean 'concentration', which is a key part of its practice.

Hindus who perform yoga think that the mind is constantly 'looking around' restlessly, unable to focus on a particular thing. They believe that yoga and meditation help control the mind and body so you are always calm and have a clear mind. This allows you to focus on truly important things and achieve a better reincarnation, or even moksha.

How do you practise yoga?

Asanas – the postures that people move their bodies into – are a key part of yoga. Some are quite simple, but others are very difficult to achieve.

Another part of yoga is pranayama, meaning 'breath control'. Being aware of and in control of your breathing is important in yoga, as it can calm you down and make it easier to concentrate and meditate. Some Hindus believe that people have a spiritual energy or force within them, which can be developed through pranayama.

A third part of yoga is dhyana, meaning 'meditation'. Meditation can involve concentrating on one object without letting anything else distract you, or trying to have no thoughts at all for a long period of time, which is very difficult! Many Hindus believe that for yoga to be successful it needs to involve all three of the elements above. Without meditation, your mind will still be distracted, and you will continue to be reincarnated.

These women are sitting in the 'sukhasana' posture. This is a simple and relatively comfortable position that is good for meditation.

Ascetics

Ascetics are people who have chosen to live their lives without the everyday comforts we are used to. In India, ascetics often live outside, or continually travel from one place to another. They eat only simple food and often fast for long periods. They have few possessions and clothes, and they tend to live by begging. Hindus believe that they can gain good karma by giving ascetics food or other help.

Some Hindu ascetics believe that their lifestyle will generate a lot of **tapas**, which means 'heat' in Sanskrit. Tapas purifies the mind and body.

By fasting intensively or staying in difficult yoga postures for a long time, a person can generate purifying tapas. This purity brings people closer to moksha. Through the ages, many Hindus have taken up yoga and meditation to achieve this.

This Hindu man from India is living as an ascetic. He is practising yoga by adopting a difficult asana, or posture.

> 66 By meditating on a pure inner light, free from pain, the mind becomes stable and calm. Or by meditating on having no desire for material objects, the mind becomes stable and calm. 99
>
> From the Yoga Sutras, a short text by the yogin Patanjali

Feature

The legend of Vishvamitra

There are many examples in Hindu myths of men and women who gain extraordinary powers because they follow an ascetic lifestyle. In the Ramayana, a man named Vishvamitra is said to have built up massive power and great abilities by meditating and fasting at the top of the Himalayas. He ate nothing (and barely breathed) for a thousand years as he tried to become a Rishi. Vishvamitra was not always perfect, and he is said to have once used his ascetic powers to turn a beautiful lady into a stone for 10,000 years because she disturbed his meditation! Despite this, Vishvamitra's asceticism led to him being respected as a truly great Rishi. He became famous for using his yogic powers for good, and often helped people in need.

The beautiful Menaka distracts Vishvamitra from his meditation. He was famously irritable and turned her to stone on the spot!

Key vocabulary

ascetic Someone who lives a simple life away from society, usually to become closer to the supreme being or to achieve moksha (also known as a sadhu)

tapas Literally 'heat'; ascetics and people practising yoga intensively generate tapas

yoga Controlling the mind and body to purify yourself and achieve moksha

Check your understanding

1. Explain what the word 'yoga' means and why it is important to Hindus.
2. Describe three parts of yoga.
3. Explain what an ascetic lifestyle involves and why people choose to follow it.
4. How did Vishvamitra use the powers he gained from living an ascetic life?
5. 'The most spiritual life is an ascetic life.' Do you agree?

Unit 1: History and belief
Extraordinary individuals

Who are some of the extraordinary individuals who inspire Hindus?

Manu

Manu was a legendary holy man who lived in the distant past. His story can be found in the Matsya (Fish) Purana. At the time of Manu, humans had become evil, so Vishnu descended to earth as a small fish. In the story, the fish asks Manu to save it from the larger fish in its small pond. Manu shows compassion and cares for the fish himself, even though it grows so large that it needs to be housed in a river, and then outgrows even that.

Kind and caring as ever, Manu carries the fish to the ocean. As he does so, the fish reveals itself as Vishnu and declares that a great flood is going to wipe out humanity because of all the evil in the world. The fish tells Manu to build a ship that will save him and his family. Manu does this and Vishnu, still in the form of a giant fish, tows the ship through the raging waters.

When the flood is over, Manu's sacrifices to Vishnu enable him to repopulate the world. Hindus believe that Manu's devotion to God, and his compassion for his fellow creatures, are what saved humanity from extinction. He is still seen as an example to Hindus today.

The Matsya avatar of Vishnu tows Manu's boat to safety.

Shankara (CE 788–820)

Shankara lived in India around 1300 years ago. He became an ascetic when he was a teenager and went begging from door to door. One day, he knocked on the door of an old woman. Although she was poor, she did not want to send a holy man away with nothing, so she gave him her last piece of fruit. When Shankara realised how poor the woman was, he composed a hymn to Lakshmi, the goddess of wealth. The poor woman's devotion and Shankara's hymn delighted the goddess and the woman was rewarded with a shower of golden fruit.

Shankara's disciples learning from their guru.

Later in Shankara's life, he travelled around India and became renowned for his intelligence. He set up several monasteries and schools of Hindu philosophy. Shankara's love of learning and his humble devotion to God remain a powerful inspiration to many Hindus today.

Caitanya (1486–1534)

Like Shankara, Caitanya was very successful in his studies. He became a teacher at the age of 16 and was very proud of his academic achievements. However, his life changed after meeting a guru in northern India. Caitanya became devoted to Krishna, a form of Vishnu, and changed the way he lived. He was no longer puffed up with pride at his academic studies. Instead, he became convinced that the best way to live was to worship Krishna constantly. Caitanya worshipped by dancing, singing loudly, and laughing and jumping with joy at the thought of Krishna. Caitanya would be in **ecstasy** when he meditated on Krishna's loving, playful character.

Caitanya and disciples dancing. Note the contrast with Shankara and his disciples!

As Caitanya's style of worshipping Vishnu became popular, some more traditional Hindus complained to the local ruler, who was a Muslim, that Caitanya was causing trouble. According to legend, Caitanya and his followers responded to this by peacefully marching to the ruler's palace to speak to him. At Caitanya's kind, loving words, the ruler wept. He then joined Caitanya's followers in a song accompanied by a devotional dance.

Caitanya believed that bhakti was the best way to live, and his teaching and life inspired many Hindus. Even today, his emotional and ecstatic style of worship is followed in some Hindu communities, and he is a particularly revered saint among Vaishnavas.

Mata Amritanandamayi Devi (b. 1953)

Mata Devi, also known as Amma ('mother'), has become famous around the world as a great Hindu spiritual leader. From a young age, she was inspired to embrace people who appeared to be sad or in need of comfort. She resisted her parents' attempts to arrange a marriage for her because she wanted to serve humanity with all her strength. Her unconditional love and service to others inspired many Hindus to become her disciples. People began to travel from all parts of the world to receive a hug from her. Even non-Hindus who receive her hug and blessing describe it as an extraordinarily warm and moving experience.

Amma is now a revered guru and her charity donates millions of pounds a year to causes like disaster relief. Amma also promotes tolerance of different faiths.

Amma giving a hug to a follower. The man might have had to queue for hours to meet her.

Key vocabulary

ecstasy An extreme feeling of happiness and joy

Check your understanding

1. Why do Hindus see Manu as a good person?
2. Describe what happened when Shankara visited the old woman.
3. Describe the way that Caitanya worshipped Vishnu.
4. Explain the differences between Shankara and Caitanya.
5. Why might Hindus see Amma as an important spiritual teacher?

Unit 1: History and belief
Knowledge organiser

Key vocabulary

ascetic Someone who lives a simple life away from society, usually to become closer to the supreme being or to achieve moksha (also known as a sadhu)

Aum A sacred syllable or sound that is very important to Hindus and which they chant

avatar A god who descends to earth as a human or other animal in order to fight evil and re-establish goodness

bhakti A Sanskrit word meaning 'devotion' or 'worship'; some Hindus believe that bhakti alone can be a way to achieve moksha

Brahman A supreme being in which most modern Hindus believe; the source of everything, including the gods

chakra A word meaning 'wheel', one of the weapons that Hindu gods may carry

deity A god or goddess

dharma The moral law that Hindus must follow; the word can be translated as 'duty' or 'righteousness'

ecstasy An extreme feeling of happiness and joy

karma The forces that influence people's fortune and future reincarnation

Mahabharata An epic story that is inspirational for Hindus

meditation The practice of focusing the mind

moksha Escaping from samsara and never dying or becoming reincarnated again; the term literally means 'release'

monotheist Someone who believes in only one god

polytheistic Referring to belief in many gods; someone who believes in many gods is a polytheist

Purana A Hindu text that is more recent than the Vedas, but is still thought to contain profound wisdom and teachings

Ramayana An epic story that is inspirational for Hindus

reincarnated When a soul is reborn by passing into a new body

Rishis The Vedic people who first heard the Vedas and taught them to others

sacrifice A method of worship that involves offering animals or food to the gods

samsara The continual process of death and reincarnation; also, the entire universe as we know it

sanatana dharma Eternal dharma or law; this never changes and is always good, regardless of the time and place

Sanskrit A language used in ancient India, which many Hindu texts are written in

Shaiva A Hindu who believes that Shiva is the Supreme God

shruti A word referring to religious teachings that are revealed to Rishis directly from God

symbol An image that expresses religious ideas

tapas Literally 'heat'; ascetics and people practising yoga intensively generate tapas

Trimurti A term for the three main Hindu gods Brahma, Vishnu and Shiva

trishula A word meaning 'three spears', another weapon symbolising the power and authority of the gods

upanayana A traditional Hindu ceremony that children undergo when they are ready to be educated about the Vedas and other sacred texts

vahana An animal 'vehicle' that transports Hindu deities

Vaishnava A Hindu who believes that Vishnu is the Supreme God

Vedas A collection of sacred writings, literally meaning 'knowledge'

vibhuti The three white lines on Shiva's forehead, which represent his superhuman powers

yoga Controlling the mind and body to purify yourself and achieve moksha

Key facts

- The roots of Hinduism can be traced back to India more than 4000 years ago. Today, it has nearly one billion followers worldwide.

- Hinduism has no single founder and no particular leader or group of leaders. Its followers, known as Hindus, have many different beliefs.

- The main sacred texts in Hinduism are the four Vedas, which are believed to have been revealed by God.

- Other important texts for Hindus include the Mahabharata, the Ramayana and the Puranas, all of which contain stories about the gods and goddesses.

- Vaishnavas believe that Vishnu is the Supreme God; Shaivas believe that Shiva is the Supreme God. Local gods are often believed to be forms or extensions of the Supreme God.

- Hinduism is rich in symbolism. Objects such as the chakra (wheel), conch shell and lotus flower all have special meanings for Hindus.

- Hindus believe in reincarnation. What determines a person's next life is karma: whether a person performs good or bad deeds in this life.

- The journey of the soul through these reincarnations is called samsara. Hindus try to achieve a permanent release from samsara known as moksha. Moksha might be achieved through yoga and meditation or through worship and devotion.

- 'Dharma' is a universal law, meaning 'duty' or 'righteousness', which guides how Hindus live their lives. They try to show loyalty and respect and support charities to help those in need.

- Yoga and meditation are ways of controlling the body and mind to help achieve moksha. They involve moving the body in certain postures (asana), controlling breathing (pranayama) and focusing the mind so it is free of distractions.

- Ascetics are Hindus who choose to give up everyday comforts and live lives of hardship, often as beggars, to purify themselves and help them towards moksha.

Key people and gods

Agni The Vedic god of fire who consumed the food offered in sacrifices and made it acceptable to other gods

Arjuna A heroic character in the Mahabharata who obeys Krishna by fighting against his own family in order to follow dharma

Brahma One of the main three Hindu gods; the creator of the world

Brahman A supreme being in which most modern Hindus believe; the source of everything, including the gods

Caitanya An exuberant worshipper of Krishna who lived from 1486 to 1534

Ganesha The elephant-headed god of wisdom

Indra The Vedic god of sky, who sent thunderbolts to earth

Kalki A warrior on a white horse; the form that Hindus believe the final avatar of Vishnu will take

Krishna One of the avatars of Vishnu; a charioteer who instructs Arjuna how to live a good life. He is a very popular deity

Lakshmi The god Vishnu's wife; the goddess of wealth

Manu A legendary man saved by the fish avatar of Vishnu

Mata Devi (Amma) A modern Hindu teacher who people travel to receive a hug from

Parvati The god Shiva's wife; a goddess of love and fertility

Rama King in the Ramayana whose wife Sita is abducted by Ravana; he defeats Ravana

Ravana The many-armed demon who abducted Sita

Rudra A much-feared Vedic god who inflicted illness upon farm animals

Shankara An intelligent ascetic who lived 1300 years ago

Shiva One of the main three Hindu gods; the destroyer of the world

Sita The wife of Rama in the Ramayana kidnapped by Ravana

Vishnu One of the main three Hindu gods; the preserver of the world

Vishvamitra A character in the Ramayana who had built up massive power and great abilities by meditating and fasting

Hinduism in the modern world

The world today is almost unrecognisable from 3000 years ago, when Hinduism was first developing. Hinduism is now a global religion with populations of Hindus in every part of the world. These Hindus have developed their own, local, forms of Hinduism. In the second half of the book, you will explore some of the issues that Hinduism has had to confront: the rise of environmental problems, controversies about discrimination based on class and gender, and whether violence and war can ever be justified. You will also examine the colourful and fascinating ways that Hindus express their devotion to their gods and goddesses in the modern world. Lastly, you will have the chance to consider how Hinduism has profoundly influenced Western culture and language.

Hinduism has inspired people to create beautiful architecture, music, literature and art. It has influenced emperors, kings and queens and shaped the traditions and cultures of many countries – even those now following a different religion. Studying religion often reveals important aspects of what it is to be human. As you find out more about Hinduism over the past 3000 years, you will gain a greater understanding of the past, the modern world and the lives of people around the world who call themselves Hindu.

2

Unit 2: Hinduism in the modern world
Forms and places of worship

How do Hindus express their devotion in worship?

Puja

In Vedic times, Hindu worship often involved public sacrifices of animals or food. Today, these only happen in a small number of Hindu communities. Most Hindu homes have a shrine in them and Hindus perform **puja**, or worship, at home. These shrines usually contain an image of the deity or deities that are most important to that particular family. Offerings of flowers, fruit and coconuts are placed in front of the images. These offerings keep alive the tradition of Hindu sacrifice that goes back over 3000 years. Hindus often also recite **mantras** at home every day.

A shrine in a Hindu home.

❝ This is the Gayatri Mantra, a very famous mantra that some Hindus chant in the morning at sunrise.

om bhur bhuvaḥ svaḥ
tát savitúr váreṇyaṁ
bhárgo devásya dhīmahī
dhíyo yó naḥ prachodayat

('We meditate on the supremely radiant glory of the divine Light; may he inspire our understanding.') **❞**
Rig Veda 3.62.10[11] (translated by S. Radhakrishnan)

Murti and darshan

The image of a deity found at a Hindu shrine or temple is called a **murti**, which means 'form' or 'image'. Whether in a temple or a home, the murti is a sacred object. A murti is not a deity itself – it is just an image of the deity. However, Hindus believe that if it is produced and installed in the right way then the murti has a special connection to the deity.

The word **darshan** is used to describe a special way of seeing a murti. In darshan, a Hindu focuses on the murti in a particular, devoted way, making this 'seeing' an act of worship. Hindus believe that by seeing the murti in this way, they will receive blessings and a sort of energy or force from the deity. In temples, murtis are usually hidden behind a curtain most of the time, but if people go to the temple at the right time darshan will be given. This means that the murti will be briefly revealed so that people can express their devotion to the deity.

This murti is in a temple to Venkateshwara, a form of Vishnu, in India. The priests treat it with great reverence.

Sometimes, darshan can also be of a holy man or woman. Hindus might travel to receive darshan from a holy person. Seeing such a person provides an opportunity to express devotion to the deity to which the holy man or woman has dedicated their life. Hindus believe that it is important to be clean and well-presented when receiving darshan, so they often wash beforehand. Hindus believe that if they are standing in the presence of a murti, they are, in a way, standing in the presence of God, so this is definitely a time to dress up!

Mandirs

Some Hindus worship regularly at a temple while others might just visit during festivals or on other special occasions. Some Hindu temples in Asia are more than 1500 years old, but there are many more modern temples. Hindu temples are sometimes called **mandirs**. Much thought goes into building mandirs. For example, they are sometimes planned on a grid of 64 squares, which is considered a particularly sacred number. This is because it is the square of eight, and some deities are considered to have eight powers or eight forms.

In many temples, the space in the very centre is the most sacred part, and is often where the murti is kept. All the other features of the temple, such as statues and altars, are arranged around the centre. This is seen as mirroring the universe, because the whole universe, including demons, humans, gods, heavens and hells, revolve around the Supreme Deity.

Sometimes Hindus bring special offerings such as colourful flowers to the temple to offer as puja to their chosen deity.

Akshardham Temple, New Delhi. The different levels of the building represent the different levels of the universe, with God at the top.

Key vocabulary

darshan 'Seeing' God; a form of worship and devotion in which the murti of a deity is revealed to worshippers

mandir A Hindu term for a temple

mantra An extract from a sacred text that is chanted repeatedly during worship

murti An image of a god or goddess

puja The Sanskrit word for worship

Check your understanding

1 What is puja?
2 What religious activities do Hindus perform in the home?
3 What is a murti?
4 Why is darshan important for Hindus?
5 Explain how Hindu temples or mandirs are built in a symbolic way.

Unit 2: Hinduism in the modern world
Places of pilgrimage

Pilgrimages are long and difficult journeys. Why do Hindus undertake them?

Pilgrimage is important to Hindus, and they make journeys to many different places for worship. Pilgrimage sites are known as **tirtha**, which means 'crossing place'. This is because a tirtha is a place where gods or goddesses are believed to come to earth to defeat evil or to become part of the world.

Varanasi

For many Hindus, the city of Varanasi in India, which has more than 200 temples, is an important pilgrimage destination. It lies on the banks of the river Ganges (Ganga in Sanskrit), which has been sacred to Hindus for thousands of years. Ganga is worshipped as a goddess. In Hindu myths, Brahma ordered Ganga to descend to earth so that the many sons of a great king could achieve moksha. Ganga was annoyed at this request and hurled herself to earth with the intention of washing it away. Shiva caught Ganga in his matted hair and this saved all life on earth. As Ganga trickled through the locks of Shiva's hair, she landed softly, forming the river Ganges. Hindus believe that bathing in the Ganges removes bad karma from past acts.

Hindus also believe that Varanasi is one of the best places on earth for their ashes to be scattered after they pass away. Having your ashes scattered in the Ganges is believed to be beneficial for your next reincarnation and brings you closer to achieving moksha. In Varanasi there are many locations along the river where devout Hindus' bodies can be cremated on a traditional funeral pyre and scattered in the sacred waters of the river.

The smoke in this picture is from a funeral pyre on the edge of the sacred river Ganges, in Varanasi.

Puri

The ancient city of Puri is the centre of devotion to a form of Vishnu known as Jagannath. Pilgrims have visited the city for centuries, and today millions of Hindus make the journey every year. One of the many attractions in Puri is the temple of Jagannath, built over 800 years ago. The temple has two large chakras on its towers, which represent the unimaginably powerful weapon that Vishnu wields. Darshan is given every day in the temple, when people are allowed to see the jewelled throne on which the murtis of the deities sit. There are over 100 shrines in the temple, so pilgrims can also show their devotion by walking around the temple and performing puja at one of these.

The Temple of Jagannath.

The Kumbh Mela

The **Kumbh Mela** is one of the largest gatherings anywhere in the world. It is a festival that takes place every three years. The location of the Kumbh Mela alternates between four different venues in India so that each location hosts the festival once every twelve years. Up to 30 million pilgrims can descend on the Kumbh Mela in a single day! During this pilgrimage, people bathe in the sacred rivers of India, including the Ganges, in order to get rid of bad karma.

A procession of sadhus at the Kumbh Mela in 2013, at Allahabad.

The Kumbh Mela is also famous for attracting many ascetics, or sadhus, who often make the pilgrimage in large groups. For ordinary Hindus, the chance to see these sadhus is an important reason to make a Kumbh Mela pilgrimage. The sight of a holy man or woman is darshan; it is considered a blessing to have the chance to see such people, and many Hindus make offerings to them or ask for spiritual advice. Putting up with the heat and crowded conditions at the Kumbh Mela in order to bathe in the Ganges and see the sadhus is what pilgrimage is about for many Hindus.

Activity

Create a brochure that provides Hindus with information about popular pilgrimage sites.

Key vocabulary

Kumbh Mela Hindu festival when ascetics bathe in a river to remove karma; it takes place every three years

tirtha A 'crossing place' where a deity enters the human world; for this reason, they are places of pilgrimage

Fact

In the Mahabharata epic, which is over 2000 years old, Arjuna goes on a pilgrimage to the river Ganges. By visiting tirthas, Hindus are continuing a tradition contained in some of the most ancient stories in the world.

Check your understanding

1. What does the word 'tirtha' mean?
2. Why do many Hindus believe that the river Ganges is sacred?
3. What do Hindus believe about Varanasi?
4. Explain why Hindus would want to see a sadhu.
5. 'The journey is the most important part of Hindu pilgrimage.' Discuss this statement.

Unit 2: Hinduism in the modern world
Hindu festivals

What are the meanings of Hindu festivals?

Hundreds of Hindu festivals are celebrated around the world. They allow Hindus to step out of ordinary life and celebrate their religion and its traditions. However, because Hinduism has developed differently in different parts of the world, Hindus do not all celebrate the same festivals.

Diwali

Diwali is a five-day festival celebrated by almost all Hindus. The timing of Diwali is based on the Hindu lunar calendar. This means that it takes place at a different time each year in the UK, but it normally falls near the end of October or the start of November. During Diwali, Hindus light many lamps and candles, so it is sometimes called the 'festival of lights'.

Diwali decorations in Leicester, UK.

Today, Diwali has different meanings for different Hindus. For some, the glow of lights at Diwali symbolises the sun's nourishing energy, and is a reminder to Hindus of their dependence on the Supreme Deity who created this world, sustains it and will eventually destroy it. Another reason why some Hindus light lamps at Diwali is to help Lakshmi, the goddess of wealth, enter their homes and bring them good fortune.

Other Hindus remember the events of the Ramayana at Diwali. For them, the lights are a reminder of Rama and Sita returning home after defeating the demon Ravana (see page 16). They arrived at Ayodhya on a moonless night. In order to guide the couple home and welcome them, the people of the city lit lamps. For many Hindus, therefore, Diwali is partly about celebrating the victory of good over evil.

Some see Diwali as a reminder of a legend from the Vedas about a good Brahmin boy called Nachiketas who meets Yama, the god of death. Yama offers to grant the boy three wishes. For his first two wishes, Nachiketas asks for peace for his family and to know more about sacrifice. For his third wish, he asks to know what happens after death. Yama is reluctant to answer this and urges Nachiketas to ask for wealth or long life. However, Nachiketas insists on an answer to his question. Yama praises Nachiketas for making a truly wise choice and explains Hindu beliefs about the soul and reincarnation to him. The lights at Diwali are thought to symbolise knowledge and wisdom defeating ignorance and darkness.

Thaipusam

Although many Hindus worship Vishnu or Shiva as the Supreme Deity, these gods take different forms. In the festival of **Thaipusam**, Shaivas worship a form of Shiva called Murugan – a fierce god of war. The festival is particularly celebrated in southern India, Malaysia, Singapore and Sri Lanka. Some devout Hindus express their devotion to Murugan by fasting for several weeks before the festival.

During Thaipusam, there are large, colourful processions of worshippers and murtis of Murugan. Some Hindus take on a **kavadi**, or 'burden', during the festival. This might mean carrying something heavy during the long Thaipusam procession to the temple. Other devotees have their faces and bodies pierced with spikes as a kavadi; others carry a huge shrine on their backs. The idea behind fasting and taking on such burdens is to show devotion to God and a willingness to sacrifice comfort and fine living for him.

A kavadi bearer in Singapore during Thaipusam.

The Ratha Yatra

The city of Puri is a popular pilgrimage site, but it also hosts a festival called the **Ratha Yatra**. 'Ratha' means 'chariot' in Sanskrit. In ancient India chariots were important in warfare and were symbols of power because warriors rode into battle in them. During the Ratha Yatra, murtis of Jagannath and other deities of the temple are placed in chariots and pulled through the city. Families spend months building the chariots from local wood in a very precise way in order to show their devotion to Jagannath.

Jagannath's 16-wheeled chariot at Ratha Yatra.

The murtis are visible for all to see during the procession, so the Ratha Yatra festival gives an opportunity for darshan. This is especially important for those unable to make it into the Jagannath temple to receive darshan there.

Key vocabulary

Diwali The festival of lights, celebrated by nearly all Hindus

kavadi A burden carried during the Thaipusam festival to express devotion to Murugan

Ratha Yatra A Vaishnava festival in Puri, involving a procession of murtis in chariots

Thaipusam A Shaiva festival to worship Murugan, the god of war

Check your understanding

1. What is Diwali often called and how long does it last?
2. Explain in detail two ways in which Diwali reminds Hindus of their beliefs and legends.
3. Explain what devotees do at Thaipusam and why.
4. Why is the Ratha Yatra important to Vaishnavas?
5. Why are there so many different Hindu festivals and why are they celebrated differently?

What is the caste system?

How have Hindu beliefs about caste changed?

According to some ancient Hindu texts, every person belonged to one of four classes, or castes. The caste that a person belonged to determined the job that he or she did. The system was intended to create a balanced community in which everyone did an important job that was required for society to function well. This way of organising society is known as the **caste system**.

From the earliest times, people viewed some castes as higher or lower than others. They also tended to believe that people were born into a caste with the qualities needed to perform a role (which meant that a person could not move between castes). They thought that following dharma meant fulfilling the duty of the person's caste. These ideas were supported by an ancient Hindu text called the Laws of Manu. The four castes, in order of how highly they were viewed, were:

These dalit women in India are using a bank designed to help rural people lift themselves out of poverty.

Brahmins: priests who looked after spiritual matters
Kshatriyas: warriors who protected society
Vaishyas: traders and farmers
Shudras: manual labourers/servants

The myth of Purusha

There is a myth about the caste system in the Rig Veda. In it, a giant called Purusha is sacrificed by the gods in order to create human society. Each caste is made from a different part of Purusha's body. The Brahmins were made from Purusha's head, showing they are thoughtful and spiritual. The Kshatriyas were made from Purusha's arms, meaning they should be strong and ready to fight against injustice. The Vaishyas were made from Purusha's thighs and the Shudras were made from his feet. Because feet are often seen as unpleasant, this could suggest that Shudras are of lower status. However, feet are also a vital part of the body, holding everything else up. As such, Hindus can interpret this myth as showing that each class is a vital and valued part of society and no caste is more important than another.

Fact

In ancient times, some Hindus even believed that Untouchables should ring a bell when they entered a village so that people could hide. This is not widely believed today.

The Untouchables

As people started to view castes as higher or lower, a fifth group developed. Members of this group were known as 'Untouchables', and no other caste would associate with them. We do not know exactly where this group came from or who became part of it, but we do know that they were regarded as lower than the Shudras. They were considered impure and had to do the most menial jobs. Unable to move caste, Untouchables faced a life of poverty and discrimination.

Activity

Prepare a case arguing either for or against the statement 'The caste system is a good thing.' Then hold a class debate.

Gandhi and the Dalits

Mohandas Gandhi is probably the most famous Hindu of the twentieth century. Gandhi taught that all Hindus are equal in God's eyes. He believed that Untouchables should be treated like any other Hindus, calling them 'Harijans', which means 'children of God'. Gandhi worked hard to end the discrimination Untouchables faced. For example, he campaigned for them to be allowed to worship inside temples, which many people were angry about. He also caused great controversy by accepting an Untouchable family a community or settlement he had developed and adopting their daughter.

The modern Indian name given to Untouchables is Dalits, which means 'oppressed' or 'broken'. Dalits prefer this term because it acknowledges that they are not really 'untouchable' and have been (and still are) oppressed. In India today, approximately 15 per cent of the population are Dalits. They still face problems in many places, and people continue to campaign to rid society of caste-based discrimination.

Gandhi speaking to Dalit workers in 1940.

The caste system today

Most modern Hindus do not think that following dharma requires people to do a specific job that they were born to do. Like Gandhi, many Hindus also believe that all human beings are of equal worth. Since 1950, laws have been passed in India to try to protect and support the lower castes. For example, there are a certain number of places reserved for non-Brahmins in schools and colleges, also for Dalits in government. Caste has not entirely disappeared in modern Indian society. Many people continue to remember their ancestral 'jati', or trade, which is a type of caste system. In some parts of rural India the caste system is also still important. Even outside India, many people still choose to marry within their own caste.

This man is a journalist from a dalit community in a slum area of Mumbai. He is showing his son a news report he produced to highlight the discrimination that dalits still face.

Key vocabulary

Caste System A series of social classes that determine someone's job and status in society

Check your understanding

1. What do Hindus think was the original intention of the caste system?
2. Explain two ways in which the myth of Purusha in the Rig Veda could be interpreted.
3. How can ideas about caste cause discrimination?
4. Explain how 'Untouchables' were treated and why they prefer the name 'Dalits'.
5. How effective have modern Hindus been at challenging caste-based discrimination? Refer to the actions of Gandhi in your answer.

Unit 2: Hinduism in the modern world
Hindu attitudes to violence

What do Hindus believe about violence?

Violence in the Vedas

It is often said that religion is a source of conflict. Some people even say that if there were no religion there would be far less conflict in the world. There are parts of the Vedas that can be seen as celebrating violence. Vedic Hindus probably feared attack from neighbouring tribes, and this is reflected in their hymns. For example, in the Rig Veda there is a hymn to the weapons of war.

However, it also says in the Vedas: 'May all beings look at me with a friendly eye, may I do likewise, and may we look at each other with the eyes of a friend.' This shows that from early in the development of their faith, Hindus believed that harming other creatures should be avoided where possible. Some Hindus go further than this, and believe in **pantheism** – the idea that God is not only everywhere, but in everything too. As such, harming any living thing should be avoided because it is harming God. Because of these beliefs, many Hindus choose to be vegetarian, and the majority of Hindus no longer sacrifice animals to gods.

Arjuna in the Mahabharata

Hindus believe that sometimes dharma requires a person to fight. Arjuna, a legendary hero, questions Krishna about this in the Bhagavad Gita. At first, Arjuna believes that it is wrong for him to fight because it will involve killing and destruction on a large scale and he will have to fight against his own family. Krishna convinces him otherwise. Arjuna is a member of the Kshatriya (warrior) caste, and the battle is part of a war that is just. Therefore, it is his dharma to fight in the battle, despite his concerns about it. However, Krishna does say that Arjuna should perform his duty in a calm and detached manner. He shouldn't fight in the battle because he takes pleasure in fighting or killing. Rather, he should only fight because it is his duty. As such, the Bhagavad Gita says to fight only when it is absolutely necessary. It does not glorify fighting or killing.

A scene from the Bhagavad Gita showing Arjuna in battle.

Gandhi and non-violence

There is an ancient idea in Hinduism called **ahimsa**, which literally means 'non-injury' or 'no harm'. This means that Hindus try to resolve conflict peacefully and show kindness to other creatures. One of the most famous modern examples of ahimsa comes from Gandhi. In the first part of the twentieth century, India was part of the British Empire, but Gandhi believed it should be a country in its own right, so he began a long but peaceful campaign to win independence for India. Even when his followers were arrested or attacked by their opponents, they would not retaliate, hurl insults or show any other aggression. Instead, they refused to follow instructions from the authorities, went on strike and fasted. Through peaceful methods, they tried to persuade the Indian population and the British authorities that it was time for India to be independent. Eventually, they succeeded.

Gandhi believed that it is better to convince people of the truth of your ideas than to force ideas on an opponent using violence. He felt that following ahimsa allowed the justice, truth and goodness of his campaign to be clearly seen by the authorities. By using ancient Hindu ideas about ahimsa, Gandhi achieved a modern political goal. Many Hindus greatly respect him for this reason and he is often called 'Mahatma' Gandhi, which means 'great soul'.

> 66 Non violence… is a weapon for the brave. 99
> Mohandas Gandhi

Fact

Ahimsa is also part of yoga. Yogins seek to control emotions like anger, hatred and aggression because no one can reach moksha if unable to control these things. As such, yogins try to be peaceful and perfectly calm. They see violent people as being unable to control themselves, and therefore a long way from moksha.

Key vocabulary

ahimsa Literally 'non-harming' or 'non-violence'; a Hindu teaching that encourages peaceful resolution of conflict and kindness towards other living creatures

pantheism The belief that God is in everything

Mahatma Gandhi under arrest. He refused to resist arrest or to allow his followers to use violence to rescue him.

Check your understanding

1 Describe Vedic ideas about violence.

2 What is pantheism?

3 What advice does Krishna give Arjuna in the Bhagavad Gita?

4 Explain how Gandhi put the idea of ahimsa into practice.

5 Why is ahimsa important to yogins?

Unit 2: Hinduism in the modern world
Do Hindus believe in gender equality?

Do Hindu women have a different role from men?

Vedic India

Ancient India was a **patriarchal society**, and men and women had very different roles. Typically, men were leaders, while women were expected to become experts at looking after their homes. Women were not allowed to become priests or perform sacrifices to the gods, but there were some religious duties that they were responsible for. For example, a wife was required to keep a fire continually burning at the shrine in her home.

Even today, there are very few female priests and temple leaders, and some Hindu temples in India only permit men to enter. However, in the twenty-first century, Hindus are beginning to re-examine the roles of men and women. Some modern Hindus believe that everyone should be free to choose a role and a place within society that is right for them, regardless of their gender. For example, in the past, it was mainly men who became ascetics, but now there are also female ascetics who practise yoga and other religious activities full time. These ascetics often live with others who have dedicated themselves to a spiritual life.

A female ascetic in Varanasi, Uttar Pradesh, India.

Sati

Traditionally, when Hindus die, they are cremated on an open funeral fire called a pyre. One reason for this is that Hindus believe the body is no longer significant once the soul has departed, so there is no need to preserve it. A few ancient Hindu writings mention a controversial custom called **sati**. This is when a woman whose husband has passed away throws herself on his funeral pyre so she can be with him immediately in the next life.

The Vedas and other respected sources do not mention sati and it was probably never a common practice. However, it may have happened occasionally in the history of Hinduism. In the past, Hindu widows were expected to remain single for the rest of their lives. Today, Hindus increasingly accept remarriage, and many women feel that they are able to remarry if their husband has died.

> 66 We should not think that we are men and women, but only that we are human beings, born to cherish and to help one another. 99
> Swami Vivekananda (1863–1902), a modern Hindu teacher

Ancient texts

The Laws of Manu, an ancient collection of Hindu teachings written more than 2000 years ago, is a controversial text, and some Hindus think that its teachings about women are unsuitable for the modern world. For example, the Laws of Manu state that a woman should be protected in childhood by her father, in adulthood by her husband and in old age by her sons. Some Hindus think that this shows respect to women by encouraging men to protect them. However, others think that the teaching stops women living independent lives.

The oldest Hindu texts are called the Vedas. It is difficult to know exactly who composed the Vedas because they were written down more than 2500 years ago, but it is likely that most of them were composed by men. However, in the oldest of the four Vedas, the Rig Veda, some hymns and poems are written by people who have what seem to be female names. Some modern Hindus see this as evidence that even in Vedic times women were viewed as wise and were respected in religious matters. There are also Hindu texts that mention women who were excellent at yoga, meditation and teaching. Therefore, some Hindus argue that women should have an important role in religious matters today. They say that dharma depends on the individual, not on gender.

Fact

Hindu women often have a coloured dot on the middle of their forehead. This is called a bindi. In the past, the bindi was a way that women showed that they were happily married. Nowadays, it is sometimes a way of showing wellbeing, or it can be a way of marking the 'third eye', which is viewed as one of the body's energy points.

Key vocabulary

patriarchal society A culture that is dominated or controlled by men

sati When a woman throws herself on to her husband's funeral pyre

Check your understanding

1. How was society patriarchal in Vedic times?
2. How are attitudes towards gender changing in Hinduism?
3. What is sati? Explain Hindu views on it.
4. Why are the Laws of Manu controversial?
5. 'Men and women should have different roles in society.' Discuss this statement with reference to Hinduism.

What are Hindu attitudes to the environment?

Can ancient teachings show Hindus how to respond to environmental problems?

Earth as a goddess

In Hindu writings, the earth is often referred to as a goddess called **Bhumi Devi** or 'Mother Earth'. Mother Earth is bountiful and provides humans with everything they need. Another way of referring to the earth is **dharti**, meaning 'she who holds everything'. Hindus believe that the earth is sacred and should be treated with respect, care and love. Causing damage to the environment is an act of disrespect to Bhumi Devi, while repairing and improving the environment shows great love and respect for her.

The battle for the heavens

At the start of the Mahabharata, there is a story about a battle between the gods and the demons over who should get to live in the heavens. The demons lost, so began to be born on earth. So many demons were born that the earth could not support all the creatures on it, as swarms of them exploited its natural resources and the animals that lived there.

Eventually, Bhumi Devi went to the god Brahma, the creator of the world, to ask for help. Brahma told the other gods to descend to earth to destroy the demons, restoring harmony and balance to Bhumi Devi. Some Hindus see this story as a very old example of taking care of our planet and a warning against taking the earth's resources for granted.

Wall mural of Goddess of Earth, Bhumi Devi.

> 66 Mother Bhumi, may whatever I dig from you grow back again quickly, and may we not injure you by our labour. 99
>
> Atharvaveda

> ### Fact
>
> Many Hindus view cows as particularly sacred creatures, and slaughtering or eating them is illegal in many parts of India. Cows are sometimes seen as a symbol of the earth and representative of all other creatures.

The Chipko movement

The Chipko movement has inspired many Hindus to take an interest in the environment. This began in the 1960s when women in a rural part of India called Gopeshwar became concerned that forests in the area were being chopped down. For hundreds of years, local people had depended on the forests for survival, and they believed the trees were sacred. They saw it as their duty to preserve them for future generations and to maintain a balance in the local environment, so they decided to protest.

Women in the Chipko movement hugged trees for days – sometimes weeks – to stop them being cut down. These women gained the support of other villagers and successfully, but peacefully, confronted armed police, violent woodcutters and local politicians to prevent their forests being destroyed. Eventually, the prime minister of India was convinced to ban the cutting down of trees in certain areas.

Green Pilgrimage Network

A pilgrimage is a journey to a holy place. People often return from pilgrimages refreshed and more committed to their religion. Pilgrimages have been popular among Hindus for 2000 years, but in the last century more Hindus than ever have travelled to holy sites in India. One popular site is the city of Puri with its temple to Jagannath. It was built over 800 years ago and attracts millions of pilgrims every year. When thousands or millions of people make the same pilgrimage in a short space of time, the environmental impact can be huge. Places like Puri suffer from litter, lack of water, air pollution from vehicles and many other problems.

Some Hindus are keen to make sure that pilgrimages have as little impact on the environment as possible. In recent years, Hindus have set up the Green Pilgrimage Network. They try to reduce the number of vehicles around temples in Puri. They also clean up gardens and areas of natural beauty and develop green energy sources for temples and pilgrimage sites. They do this because they believe that devotion to gods or goddesses should not come at the expense of Bhumi Devi.

Women of the Chipko movement protecting a tree.

Activity

Design a leaflet that raises awareness among Hindus of the importance of looking after the environment. Your leaflet should:

- explain why Hindus should care about the environment
- describe an example of inspirational work
- explain what Hindus can do or are doing to help the environment.

Millions of pilgrims visit Puri every year for religious festivals. The environmental impact can be significant.

Key vocabulary

Bhumi Devi 'Mother Earth' – earth seen as a goddess

dharti 'She who holds everything' – a way of referring to the earth goddess

Check your understanding

1. Explain why Hindu beliefs about reincarnation might lead them to want to protect the environment.
2. Why do Hindus believe that the earth is special?
3. What happens in the story about demons at the start of the Mahabharata?
4. Describe how the Chipko movement helped to protect the environment.
5. 'Hindu beliefs help to protect the environment.' Discuss this statement.

Unit 2: Hinduism in the modern world
Hinduism in world culture

How have Hindu ideas influenced world culture?

Hinduism in Western culture

Some words in the English language have been part of Hinduism for a long time. For example, 'karma' is an idea found in Hindu culture for over 2500 years, but it is now fairly common to hear it used even by non-Hindus. 'Yoga' is similarly old. Yoga was once mainly practised by ascetics, with the aim of achieving moksha. Today, however, non-Hindus around the world practise yoga and meditation. Yoga has become a popular way for people of all religions to relax, get fit and stay healthy.

A genetically engineered avatar from the 2009 film Avatar.

The words 'mantra' and 'guru' are also sometimes used in English. A mantra is a sacred phrase repeated by Hindus. In English, it is used to describe a phrase or motto that someone lives by. In Sanskrit, 'guru' means a respected teacher. In English, 'guru' describes someone who is an expert on a certain subject. Look online and you will find management 'gurus' and marketing 'gurus'. Your teacher may even have met education 'gurus'!

Sometimes people use the word 'avatar' to mean a picture that is chosen to represent a player in a game or on social media on the internet. Film director James Cameron was inspired by the Hindu idea of an avatar when writing and directing his 2009 film Avatar. In the movie, a human's intelligence and consciousness is implanted into a genetically engineered alien body in order to communicate with aliens on a planet that humans cannot inhabit. Avatar is a science-fiction film about humans hundreds of years in the future, inspired by a very ancient idea.

The Mahabharata on screen

In India, the Mahabharata has inspired several film and television shows. It is difficult to tell the entire story of the Mahabharata, as it contains over 1.8 million words, but in 1988 an Indian television series called *Mahabharat* attempted to do this. It ran for 94 episodes over 2 years and was incredibly popular. For many Hindus, it was inspiring to see the eternal battle between good and evil recreated on television. The series was so successful that it was also shown in the UK.

The Mahabharata and Ramayana in puppets and dance

In ancient times, Hindu myths and stories were often performed on stage through song and dance. In Indonesia, a type of puppet theatre called Wayang developed. Traditional Wayang theatre is still performed in

Indonesia today. Beautiful puppets are used to perform traditional Hindu stories such as the Mahabharata or Ramayana. Often, the puppets are not directly seen – instead, they are used to create shadows on a piece of white cloth, with light provided by an oil lamp. The stories are narrated by a dalang, a performer skilled at using his or her voice to convey the drama and emotion of the epic stories. An orchestra provides musical accompaniment.

These puppets are in a traditional Wayang shadow puppet show of a story from the Mahabharata.

In Thailand, most people are Buddhists, not Hindus. However, there is a traditional form of theatre called Khon, which involves performing stories from the Thai version of the Ramayana, the Ramakien. Khon theatre is performed by dancers who often wear masks and elaborate, shining costumes. They practise for years to learn the graceful dance movements that express the story. The Ramakien gives a larger role to Hanuman and his army of monkeys than the Ramayana does, and their costumes on stage are particularly dramatic. The Mahabharata and Ramayana present such powerful stories of good triumphing over evil that they have proved popular around the world for over 2000 years.

The dancer in the centre is Hanuman in this Thai Khon theatre production of stories from the Ramayana.

Hinduism around the world

Hinduism has influenced the culture of the world for millennia. It has touched non-Hindu cultures and produced some of the world's greatest art, architecture and literature. Because Hinduism has such a rich culture, it is also highly diverse. If there is one lesson to take away from studying Hinduism, it is to realise how different it can be around the world. Its culture is wide, rich and fascinating.

Activity

Draw a table and list as many similarities and differences as you can between Hinduism and any other religion that you have studied.

Check your understanding

1. Give three examples of words that have entered English from Sanskrit and Hinduism.
2. Why has yoga become popular among non-Hindus?
3. Explain what an avatar is in Hinduism and in the 2009 film.
4. Describe how the Mahabharata and Ramayana are portrayed in Indonesia and Thailand.
5. Using ideas from this book, discuss why Hinduism might be said to be 'diverse'.

Knowledge organiser

Key vocabulary

ahimsa Literally 'non-harming' or 'non-violence', a Hindu teaching that encourages peaceful resolution of conflict and kindness towards other living creatures

caste system A series of social classes that determine someone's job and status in society

darshan 'Seeing' God; a form of worship and devotion in which the murti of a deity is revealed to worshippers

dharti 'She who holds everything' – a way of referring to the earth goddess

Diwali The festival of lights, celebrated by nearly all Hindus

kavadi A burden carried during the Thaipusam festival to express devotion to Murugan

mandir A Hindu term for a temple

mantra An extract from a sacred text that is chanted repeatedly during worship

murti An image of a god or goddess

pantheism The belief that God is in everything

patriarchal society A culture that is dominated or controlled by men

puja The Sanskrit word for worship

Ratha Yatra A Vaishnava festival in Puri involving a procession of murtis in chariots

sati When a woman throws herself on to her husband's funeral pyre

Thaipusam A Shaiva festival to worship Murugan, the god of war

tirtha A 'crossing place', where a deity enters the human world; for this reason, tirthas are places of pilgrimage

Key facts

- Hindu worship is called puja, and it may be done at a shrine in the home or in a temple. The image of a deity in a shrine or temple is called a murti. Hindus 'see' or worship these in a special way called darshan.

- Making a pilgrimage to one of Hinduism's many holy sites is believed to create good karma. Key pilgrimage sites include Varanasi on the river Ganges and the city of Puri.

- Hindus in different parts of the world celebrate different festivals, but almost all Hindus celebrate Diwali, the festival of lights. It means different things to different people: Diwali may be to honour the Supreme Deity, or to remember the events of the Ramayana or a legend from the Vedas.

- The caste system is a social structure mentioned in some ancient Hindu texts. It divides society into four classes, which later developed into five, with the 'Untouchables', or Dalits, at the bottom. Mohandas Gandhi campaigned to stop discrimination against the Dalits, although they still face problems today.

- Hindus believe it is important to avoid harming other creatures, summed up in the ancient idea of ahisma, which means 'non-harming'.

- In ancient times, Hindu men and women had different roles in society. Although there is more gender equality today, there are still not many female Hindu priests or temple leaders.

- Hindus respect and value the earth because it provides people with everything they need to survive. For this reason, they work hard to protect it against environmental problems.

- Ancient Hindu ideas have influenced popular culture through the centuries, for example in the form of practices such as yoga and meditation, theatre shows and films.

Key people and gods

Bhumi Devi 'Mother Earth' – the earth seen as a goddess

Gandhi A Hindu who lived from 1869 to 1948 who opposed caste-based discrimination and led peaceful protests for Indian independence

Ganga A goddess who formed the river Ganges

Jagannath An important deity for many Hindus, believed to be a form of Vishnu

Murugan A fierce god of war, a form of Shiva, worshipped by Shaivas at Thaipusam

Purusha A mythical giant whose vast body was sacrificed by the gods to create human society

Yama The god of death

Murugan Golden Statue at Battuck caves, Kuala lampur, Malaysia, Asia.

Hindu priests in India worship goddess Durga during the Hindu festival of Dussera.

Buddhism

History and belief

In this book, you will find out about one of the most-followed religions in the world today – Buddhism. In the first half of this book you will discover how Buddhism started and spread. You will see how Buddhism grew from the experiences of an Indian prince called Siddhartha Gautama, who lived 2500 years ago, to a global religion followed by over 500 million people. You will also examine some of the central ideas in the religion which shape the lives of millions of people around the world who call themselves Buddhist.

Unit 1: History and belief
What is Buddhism?

Buddhism began in India more than 2500 years ago.
Who was its founder and what do Buddhists believe?

Buddhism is now the fourth-largest religion in the world. It has
approximately 500 million followers, known as Buddhists. There are
Buddhists all over the world, but the vast majority (99 per cent) live in
Asia. Approximately 200,000 Buddhists live in the UK.

How did Buddhism begin?

Buddhism began in a place called Lumbini in an area of ancient India
that is now Nepal. The founder of Buddhism was a prince called Siddhartha
Gautama, who was born around 563 BCE. In an effort to understand the truth
about life, Siddhartha practised **meditation**. Through this, he eventually
achieved **enlightenment**. Afterwards, he travelled around India, sharing what
he had learned. People who followed Siddhartha called him the **Buddha**
('awakened one') because they believed that he was awakened to the true
nature of reality.

Is the Buddha a god?

The Buddha never claimed to be a god, so, although his teachings
are important to Buddhists, they do not believe that he is divine or
that he was sent by a god. Buddhist **scriptures** do not mention a
creator god. One of the most important sacred texts in Buddhism is the
Dhammapada, which Buddhists believe is an accurate collection of the
Buddha's teachings.

Siddhartha Gautama died at the
age of 80. He remains one of the
most influential religious figures
in history.

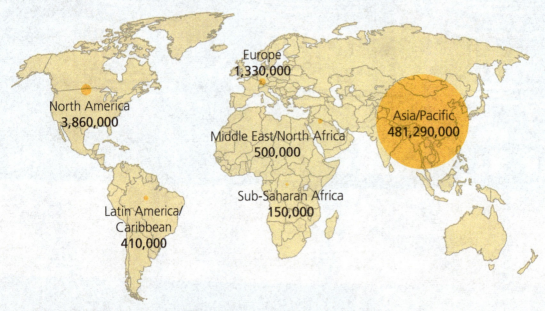

Europe
1,330,000

North America
3,860,000

Asia/Pacific
481,290,000

Middle East/North Africa
500,000

Latin America/
Caribbean
410,000

Sub-Saharan Africa
150,000

A map showing the distribution of Buddhists across the world.

What do Buddhists believe?

Unlike many other religions, Buddhists do not necessarily believe in a single creator god or gods. Instead, they focus on personal development. Buddhist temples always contain a statue of the Buddha, and Buddhists sometimes bow to this as a sign of respect, admiration and appreciation for his teachings, but they do not worship him as a god. Some Buddhists say that they pray. However, this does not mean that they pray to a god or ask for divine help. Buddhist prayer may involve personal reflection, often through chanting and making offerings.

Buddhists believe that we are travelling through a continual cycle of birth, death and rebirth. They call this cycle **samsara**. Buddhists believe that when someone dies he or she is reborn. The person's next life may be better or worse, depending on the **karma** he or she has stored up. Good actions in life store up good karma; bad actions store up bad karma. Buddhists aim to escape samsara by achieving enlightenment through meditation, wisdom and living a good life. Buddhists believe that people who escape samsara enter into a state of complete bliss called **parinirvana**.

How do we know about the Buddha?

There is much debate about the details of the Buddha's life. He lived 2500 years ago and, as far as we know, he did not write down any of his teachings or beliefs. These were passed on orally and then collected and recorded by his followers in the centuries after his death.

Many different stories about the Buddha were told and biographies were written by people living in different parts of Asia. The earliest complete biography was written in the first century CE, 500 years after the Buddha's death. Some of the details in biographies of the Buddha's life conflict with each other and historians who study them disagree about whether any of the events in his life really happened. For many Buddhists, the question of whether the events happened historically is not the most important thing. It is the message of the Buddha's life story that is most important to them.

> 66 All that we are is the result of what we have thought: it is founded on our thoughts, it is made up of our thoughts. 99
> Dhammapada chapter 1, verse 1

Key vocabulary

Buddha The awakened or enlightened one

Dhammapada A Buddhist scripture that contains the teachings and sayings of the Buddha

enlightenment The state of being awakened to the truth about life

karma The forces that influence peoples' fortune and future rebirth

meditation The practice of focusing the mind

parinirvana A state of complete bliss, entered into by souls that are not reborn

samsara The continual process of life, death and rebirth

scriptures Religious texts

Check your understanding

1 How many Buddhists are there in the world and where do they live?

2 When and where did Buddhism begin?

3 Explain who Siddhartha Gautama was and how both a historian and a Buddhist might view the events of his life.

4 Explain Buddhist beliefs about samsara.

5 Explain why there might be debate over whether Buddhism is a religion.

The early life of Siddhartha Gautama

Siddhartha Gautama was born a prince. What happened in his childhood to suggest that he was destined for a very different life?

Siddhartha's mother, Queen Maya, ruled over one of the sixteen kingdoms in ancient India. According to Buddhist legend, she had a vivid dream while she was pregnant with Siddhartha. In the dream, a white elephant gave her a beautiful lotus flower before entering into her side. The king realised that this dream was important, so he called the **Brahmins** to interpret it. The Brahmins told the king that his son would become either a great and powerful ruler who would conquer the world or a holy teacher and an enlightened being.

Siddhartha's upbringing

Soon after Siddhartha's birth, his mother died. He was raised by his aunt, who treated him as if he were her own son. Siddhartha's early life as a prince was one of luxury and indulgence. His father ensured that his son wanted for nothing, and Siddhartha grew up a healthy, intelligent and contented child.

Siddhartha and the swan

The stories of Siddhartha's early life demonstrate his wisdom and compassion. On one occasion, mentioned in an early biography of the Buddha called the Abhiniskramana Sutra, Siddhartha was playing with some friends in the palace garden. One of the boys was his cousin, Prince Devadatta. Preparing to fight in defence of the kingdom was an essential part of a prince's education, so both boys were skilled archers. While they were playing, Devadatta shot down a swan with his bow and arrow, badly wounding the bird. Devadatta wanted to keep the swan, but Siddhartha refused to give it to his cousin. Instead, he took care of it, and when it had recovered he set it free. In his later teachings, the Buddha emphasised the importance of showing compassion and loving kindness to all living things.

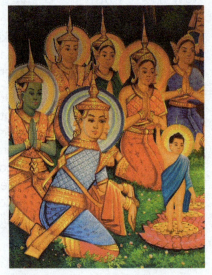

Legends say that right after birth, Siddhartha walked seven steps forward and at each step a lotus flower appeared on the ground.

Siddhartha at the ploughing ceremony

In another story from the same book, Siddhartha attended the annual ploughing ceremony. This ceremony marked the time when new crops would be sown. Following tradition, Siddhartha's father opened the ceremony by driving the first pair of prize cows across the field. The young prince Siddhartha sat down in the shade of a tree and watched everyone. The crowds were cheering and happy, but Siddhartha noticed that while people were having fun the animals were straining under

The ploughing festival, known as Raek Na, still takes place in Thailand each May and marks the start of rice-growing season.

the weight of the plough. The ploughing also brought worms to the surface, which were then eaten by birds. It struck Siddhartha that even a festival, which should be a time of happiness, caused suffering.

After noticing this, Siddhartha fell into a deep meditative trance. He breathed in and out slowly and found that he could focus his mind in a way that helped him better understand himself and the world around him. Meditation would become central to his life as the Buddha. It is a key part of Buddhism today.

> ## Fact
>
> Historians cannot be sure that these events from Siddhartha's childhood really took place. However, the fact that early Buddhists wrote these stories shows that they wanted to demonstrate that the teachings and message of Buddhism were part of Siddhartha's life even before he became known as the Buddha.

> 66 When I was a child, I was delicately brought up, most delicately. A white sunshade was held over me day and night to protect me from cold, heat, dust, dirt, and dew. My father gave me three lotus ponds: one where red lotuses bloomed, one where white lotuses bloomed, one where blue lotuses bloomed. 99
>
> The Buddha, recalling his childhood

A life of luxury

Siddhartha's father did not want his son to become a holy man as the Brahmins had suggested. He wanted him to inherit the kingdom and become a great ruler. He made sure that Siddhartha was brought up in luxury and received the best education. The king also arranged for Siddhartha to marry his cousin, Yashodhara. The royal couple were waited on by servants and only the most beautiful and healthy people in the kingdom were allowed to visit them. They ate the finest foods and wore expensive clothes. One of the many legends about the Buddha says that they spent 10 years on honeymoon in a variety of specially built palaces within the walls of the royal grounds, and Siddhartha was kept entertained by musicians and dancing girls.

Siddhartha and his wife, Yashodhara.

Yashodhara became pregnant and gave birth to a son, Rahula. The king was happy – his son's life was exactly as he had hoped. However, Siddhartha wanted to know what lay beyond the walls of the royal grounds. He asked his servant, Channa, to take him outside and show him what life was really like.

> ## Key vocabulary
>
> **Brahmins** Priests in ancient India who interpreted Queen Maya's dream when she was pregnant with Siddhartha

> ## Check your understanding
>
> **1** How did the Buddha describe his childhood when he looked back on it as an adult?
>
> **2** What does the story of the swan tell us about Siddhartha's character?
>
> **3** What lesson did Siddhartha learn by watching the ploughing festival?
>
> **4** Who were Yashodhara and Rahula?
>
> **5** Explain why the king did not want Siddhartha to leave the palace grounds and how he tried to prevent it.

Unit 1: History and belief
The Four Sights and the Great Departure

What did Siddhartha see when he left the grounds of his palace that changed his life forever?

At the age of 29, Siddhartha decided that he wanted to leave the royal grounds for the first time to see what lay beyond its walls. When the king found out that his son wanted to leave, he arranged for Siddhartha to visit one of the royal parks near the palace, but he gave instructions that anyone who was poor, elderly or ill should be kept away. The people were delighted to see their prince and they cheered as Siddhartha made his way along the roads in a chariot.

The Four Sights

The first sight: old age

The gods realised that the king was trying to deceive the future Buddha, so they transformed a member of the crowd into a white-haired old man, bent over with age. Siddhartha had never seen an elderly person before. When he asked Channa about it, Channa explained that everyone must age. Siddhartha sighed deeply, shook his head and said: 'So that is how old age destroys the memory, beauty and the strength of all!'

Siddhartha Gautama and the four sights of old-age, disease, death and an ascetic.

The second sight: sickness

On Siddhartha's next journey, the gods showed him a vision of a diseased man, wailing and groaning in pain. According to the **Pali Canon**, when Channa explained illness to the prince, Siddhartha is said to have 'trembled like the reflection of the moon on rippling water' and said: 'This then is the calamity of disease, which afflicts all. The world sees it but does not lose its confident ways.'

The third sight: death

On the third journey, Siddhartha saw a dead man's body being carried along the road in a funeral procession. The prince asked why the man was not moving and why the people following the procession were crying. Again, Channa explained the sight to him. Upon learning about death for the first time, Siddhartha was filled with dismay. He lost courage and hope, declaring: 'This is the end which has been fixed for all and yet the world forgets its fears and takes no heed.'

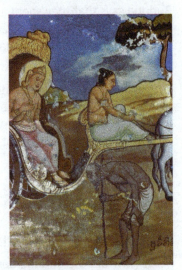

Siddhartha meets the old man.

From this moment, Siddhartha withdrew from palace life and stopped finding happiness in the luxuries provided for him. He began to think about the true meaning of life and realised that he had much to learn. 'It is not that I despise the objects of the world,' he explained. 'But when I consider the impermanence of everything in this world then I can find no delight in it.'

The fourth sight: a holy man

On his final journey, the prince rode his horse into the forest, hoping to find peace and solitude for his troubled mind. As he approached the woodland, he saw an **ascetic** man walking – almost gliding – towards him from the trees. The man wore simple robes and explained calmly to Siddhartha that he had given up his home, his possessions and his family to search for an answer to all the suffering and unhappiness in the world. The man then disappeared before the prince's eyes.

The Great Departure

Siddhartha decided that he needed to leave his life as a prince and search for an answer to the question of how to deal with the suffering in the world. He returned to the palace, took a final look at his sleeping wife and son, and then he and Channa left under the cover of night. When Siddhartha reached a refuge in the forest, he removed his jewels and his weapons. He also cut his hair and replaced his royal robes with simple clothes. Siddhartha commanded Channa to return his possessions to his father and then come back to him. Channa begged the prince not to leave, but Siddhartha replied: 'Birds settle on a tree for a while, and then go their separate ways again. Clouds meet and then fly apart again. The meeting of all living beings must likewise inevitably end in their parting.'

After witnessing the Four Sights, Siddhartha left his life of luxury behind him.

Most historians believe that the story of the **Four Sights** is probably not literally or historically true, but it still has great spiritual meaning for Buddhists.

❝ It is hard to believe that the Buddha was as naive as the story portrays him, or that his disenchantment with palace life was nearly as sudden. It might be more useful to read the story as a **parable**. ❞

Damien Keown (Professor of Buddhism), *Buddhism: A Very Short Introduction* (OUP, 2000), p. 19

Activity

Divide your page into four. In each section draw an image to represent one of the Four Sights and explain how it affected Siddhartha.

Key vocabulary

ascetic Someone who lives a life of simplicity and self-denial

Four Sights Four things seen by Siddhartha when leaving the royal grounds – old age, sickness, death and a holy man

Pali Canon The main sacred text for many Buddhists which contains the teachings of the Buddha, rules for monks and nuns and the philosophy of Buddhism; also known as the Tipitaka

parable A story used to teach a moral or spiritual lesson

Check your understanding

1. What were the Four Sights?
2. What did the Four Sights make Siddhartha realise?
3. What did Siddhartha decide to do after encountering all Four Sights?
4. Explain the meaning of Siddhartha's words to Channa about the birds and clouds.
5. 'Siddhartha did the right thing by leaving his life in the palace.' Discuss this statement.

The path to enlightenment

Siddhartha spent six years practising meditation and living as an ascetic. How did he eventually achieve enlightenment?

Siddhartha left the palace because he wanted to discover answers to the question of how to overcome suffering. He met two masters of meditation who taught him how to meditate intensively. Siddhartha was an excellent student and greatly impressed the masters, but he did not find the answers that he was looking for. He decided to set off on his own, travelling across India.

Asceticism

While travelling, Siddhartha met five ascetics by the banks of a river. When the ascetics saw how gifted Siddhartha was at meditation, they decided to become his followers. Siddhartha spent the next six years of his life living as an ascetic. Ascetics would punish their body in order to try and gain peace and wisdom. This could involve fasting, standing on one foot for a long time and sleeping on nails. Siddhartha hoped that denying his body the things it wanted would help free his mind to find the answers he was searching for.

This statue shows Siddhartha during the time when he was starving himself.

First, Siddhartha learned how to control his breath. He practised holding his breath for as long as possible, but this made him suffer from headaches and exhaustion. Next, he decided to starve himself. Buddhist legends say that he survived on only a spoonful of soup, a single seed or a single grain of rice each day. Soon, Siddhartha became ill. He was unable to stand or even sit upright, his hair fell out and his bones began to be visible through his skin. Siddhartha realised that he would die if he continued without enough food, so he decided to give up his ascetic life. His five ascetic followers found him eating and so abandoned him, thinking he loved luxury too much.

The Middle Way

Siddhartha's asceticism led him to an important truth. He realised that denying his body what it needed was as bad as being surrounded by luxury. Neither extreme brought him any closer to finding the answers he was looking for. He saw that the only way to reach peace was to follow the **Middle Way** – a life of moderation, in which he had neither too much nor too little of anything. This is a key principle that Buddhists try to live by today.

After abandoning the ascetic lifestyle, Siddhartha visited the north Indian city of **Bodh Gaya**. He was still weak from his years of self-denial. One day he went down to the river to bathe and met a young girl. She was shocked by his withered appearance and overcome by his holiness. The girl offered Siddhartha some rice milk, which he accepted willingly. The milk gave Siddhartha some strength. He put aside the rags he had been wearing and sat down, cross-legged, in the shade of a Bodhi tree. He began to meditate, saying: 'I will not move from this spot until I have found supreme and final wisdom.'

The defeat of Mara

While Siddhartha was meditating, the demon Lord Mara began to attack him. Mara sent his three daughters to tempt Siddhartha. He resisted them. Next, Mara tried to convince Siddhartha that it was wrong for him to abandon his family. Still, Siddhartha refused to move. Mara then unleashed a host of demons and monsters on Siddhartha. Still, Siddhartha did not move. Finally, Mara ordered Siddhartha: 'Arise from that seat! It belongs to me.' Siddhartha said nothing, but lowered one of his hands to touch the earth. As he did so, the sky filled with thunder and the earth shook. Mara had been defeated.

Lord Mara attacking Siddhartha.

Siddhartha was finally free to achieve his goal of enlightenment. Through deep meditation, he gained the ability to remove all greed, hatred and delusion. He had found **nirvana** and become the Buddha.

Fact

Some Buddhists interpret the story of Mara literally, as a historical event – they think that there was an actual demon spirit who tried to stop Siddhartha from meditating. Other Buddhists see Mara as a symbolic character, representing the desires and temptations of the mind that people need to remove if they are to achieve enlightenment.

The three stages of enlightenment

Siddhartha's enlightenment is said to have happened in three stages over the course of one night. During the first stage, he saw all of the many animal and human lives that he had lived before. In the second stage, he saw the complete cycle of samsara, which was like a wheel constantly spinning. Siddhartha realised that the cycle of death and rebirth of all beings in the universe is determined by their karma. In the final stage, Siddhartha achieved enlightenment.

Key vocabulary

Bodh Gaya The holiest site in Buddhism, where Siddhartha meditated under a Bodhi tree and became the Buddha

Middle Way A lifestyle between luxury and having nothing at all

nirvana A state of bliss experienced by those who have found enlightenment

Check your understanding

1. Why did Siddhartha become an ascetic?
2. Describe the methods of self-denial that Siddhartha tried.
3. What is the Middle Way?
4. Explain two different ways in which the story of Mara can be interpreted.
5. Explain how Siddhartha achieved enlightenment.

Unit 1: History and belief
The Four Noble Truths

What truths did the Buddha teach others to help them achieve enlightenment?

After Siddhartha reached enlightenment he stayed in Bodh Gaya for weeks, wondering what he should do next. He realised that he needed to share the truths that he had discovered, but did not know how best to do this.

The dharma

The Buddha said that he did not create any new ideas – he simply tried to explain how the world was. The name that Buddhists give to the laws or truths that Buddha discovered is the **dharma**. At first, the Buddha was unsuccessful in sharing the dharma. One story tells how he met a man who asked him 'Who is your teacher?' The Buddha replied that he had no teacher and had reached enlightenment on his own. The man walked away, unimpressed. This story shows that the Buddha remained an ordinary man after his enlightenment. He did not become a god.

The first sermon

After several weeks, the Buddha left Bodh Gaya and travelled 200 miles to a city called Sarnath, near the river Ganges. He came to a deer park in the city where he found the five followers who had abandoned him. They were still living as ascetics and were sceptical of their former leader's claim to have achieved enlightenment. In the deer park, the Buddha preached his first **sermon** to the five men, explaining what he had learned under the Bodhi tree. This sermon is known as 'Setting in Motion the Wheel of the Dharma' and its teachings are known as the **Four Noble Truths**, and are the basis of Buddhism.

The Four Noble Truths

1. All creatures suffer

In the first Noble Truth, Buddha taught that life is not how we would like it to be, and this causes us suffering. The **Sanskrit** word for this is dukkha. As well as suffering, dukkha is sometimes translated as dissatisfaction or stress.

The Buddha realised that even when we do find happiness it only lasts for a fleeting moment before we become dissatisfied again. He taught that many people try to ignore or deny this truth, but in order to overcome suffering they must accept it.

2. Suffering is caused by selfish desires

In the second Noble Truth, the Buddha taught that selfish desires and cravings are the cause of all suffering. This craving might be for material

> **Fact**
>
> Buddhist philosophy is underpinned by three key ideas. These are sometimes referred to as the three universal truths:
>
> - anicca – everything changes
> - anatta – there is no permanent self
> - **dukkha** – everything suffers.

A statue showing Siddhartha preaching to the five ascetics who abandoned him.

> ❝ Birth is suffering, decay, sickness and death are suffering. To be separated from what you like is suffering. To want something and not get it is suffering. ❞
>
> The Buddha

things, for people, or even for immortality. We might be temporarily satisfied, but this is short lived because everything that exists is constantly changing or turning like a wheel. Nothing is permanent, so even when our desires are fulfilled we do not gain lasting peace and satisfaction. To achieve enlightenment, therefore, we must stop allowing ourselves to be controlled by selfish desires or cravings because these desires are at odds with reality, which is always changing.

3. Suffering can be ended

The third Noble Truth is the idea that because we are the cause of our own suffering we can also overcome it and achieve enlightenment like the Buddha. Reaching nirvana requires us to eliminate all greed, hatred and delusion, which are called the **Three Poisons**.

4. The way to end suffering is to follow the Eightfold Path

In the fourth Noble Truth, the Buddha provided eight instructions for people to follow in order to be free from suffering and reach enlightenment. These instructions are known as the **Eightfold Path**. This path provides a guide to how Buddhists should live their lives.

The Buddha is seen as a guide. His teachings help people understand why we suffer.

The analogy of the doctor

One way of understanding the Four Noble Truths is through the following analogy. If you are ill then you go the doctor. The doctor will (1) see what the problem is, (2) understand its cause, (3) decide on a cure and (4) prescribe a way of making you better. This is why Buddhists sometimes think the Buddha is like a doctor whose mission is to help remove suffering from the world.

Key vocabulary

dharma The Buddha's teachings

dukkha The suffering or dissatisfaction of all living beings

Eightfold Path Eight instructions taught by the Buddha to help people overcome suffering and reach enlightenment

Four Noble Truths The basis of the Buddha's teachings: all creatures suffer; suffering is caused by selfish desires; suffering can be ended; the way to end suffering is to follow the Eightfold Path

Sanskrit An ancient Indian language

sermon A speech given by a religious leader

Three Poisons Greed, hatred and delusion

The Buddha is seen as a guide.

Check your understanding

1. What is meant by 'dharma'?
2. Why is the symbol of the wheel important to Buddhists?
3. What are the Four Noble Truths?
4. Explain each of the Four Noble Truths in your own words.
5. Explain how the analogy of the doctor helps explain the Four Noble Truths.

Unit 1: History and belief
The Eightfold Path

How does the Eightfold Path guide Buddhists on how to live in order to reach nirvana?

The Eightfold Path is not a set of rules that people must follow in order to please an almighty god. Buddhists do not believe that their actions are judged by a god. The path consists of eight steps to help people achieve a contented life. By following the Eightfold Path, Buddhists believe they can overcome the selfish desires that cause all suffering. It directs people to think, speak and act in better ways, which helps them to achieve inner peace and eliminate suffering.

The eight parts all fit together and should not be taken individually. No step is more important than any other. Buddhists believe that the steps should be developed and practised in their day-to-day lives.

The Spring Temple Buddha statue in China is one of the tallest statues in the world. The Buddha's right hand is held up with his palm facing outwards. This symbolises a shield, representing the fact that the Buddha offers protection from suffering.

The Eightfold Path

1. Right understanding

This first step in the Eightfold Path can also be translated as 'right view' and means to see things clearly and to understand them. The Buddha taught his followers that they must understand and accept the Four Noble Truths and that all living creatures are in a cycle of birth, death and rebirth (samsara).

2. Right thought

The Buddha taught that people should devote their lives to thinking in the right way in order to remove selfish desires and hatred. People should focus their mind on compassionate thoughts and developing wisdom rather than selfish thoughts that cause suffering.

3. Right speech

The Buddha taught that people should always speak truthfully and compassionately. Unkind words, swearing, lies and gossip should be avoided. This step also involves knowing when to speak and when to remain silent.

4. Right action

The fourth step is sometimes translated as 'right conduct', which means acting in the right way. The Buddha taught that people should act in a compassionate way that avoids causing harm. In particular, the Buddha said that people should avoid killing, stealing and any other action that causes harm to themselves or another living being (including animals).

5. Right livelihood

Livelihood refers to the work or job that you do to make money. The Buddha taught that people should avoid jobs that involve causing harm or encourage dishonesty.

6. Right effort

The final three steps on the path are about training your mind. Right effort means making an effort to be aware and in control of what is happening in your mind. People should limit and dispose of harmful thoughts. Instead, they should focus on positive thoughts.

7. Right mindfulness

This is sometimes translated as right awareness. People should train their mind to be fully aware of their thoughts and actions as well as being conscious of others around them. Some Buddhists talk about being aware or 'mindful' of the present moment. Buddhists try to avoid distracting thoughts about the past or the future.

8. Right concentration

To train their minds fully, people must practise meditation. Buddhists use a variety of meditation techniques in order to calm the mind, understand reality and guide them in their day-to-day lives.

The symbol of the wheel has eight spokes representing the Eightfold Path.

The analogy of the path

The Buddha taught that by following the Eightfold Path correctly people could escape the suffering experienced in samsara. The path offers a way to shape life in pursuit of wisdom, truth and virtue, and leads to a place to which, deep down, everyone wants to go. It is a path to enlightenment. The path is not a straight one, nor is it easy to navigate. Buddhists believe that people must follow the path in their own way and that they will almost certainly stumble or fall as they journey through life.

The path leading to the Buddha at Fo Guang Shan Buddha Museum, Taiwan.

Activity

Create a flow chart to summarise the Eightfold Path. Add bullet points to explain what each step requires and give examples from everyday life if you can.

Check your understanding

1 What is the Eightfold Path?
2 How does a wheel symbolise the Eightfold Path?
3 Explain each step of the path in your own words.
4 Explain how following the Eightfold Path is different from following a set of rules in another religion that you know about.
5 'The Buddha should be remembered as a great religious leader.' Discuss this statement.

Unit 1: History and belief
What is the Sangha?

As he travelled around India, the Buddha attracted many followers. How did these followers honour the Buddha and follow his teachings?

The first Buddhists

The first Buddhist community was established in Sarnath, but the Buddha and his early disciples travelled around northern India, spreading the dharma. Many people were attracted to the Buddha's message because it offered freedom from suffering. It especially appealed to lower-class people, who experienced great hardship. At the time of the Buddha, Indian society was governed by the **caste system**. Everybody belonged to a caste, which determined what sort of job they did and the kind of life they led. People were born into a caste and could not leave it. The most respected caste was priests (Brahmins). Below them were the warriors. This was the caste that the Buddha had been born into. Beneath them were farmers and then servants. At the bottom were the Untouchables: social outcasts that nobody would associate with.

The Buddha's teachings went against the caste system. He taught that caste and social hierarchy were irrelevant – all beings are part of the same cycle of samsara.

The Three Jewels

As more people began to follow the Buddha's message, a community of monks and nuns was established. This became known as the **Sangha**. The first monks, called **bhikkhus**, were the five ascetics who had previously abandoned Siddhartha, but became his followers again after his sermon in the deer park.

In the early days of Buddhism monks and nuns followed the same rules. Those who joined the Sangha were required to shave their heads, wear simple orange or yellow robes and recite the **Three Jewels** (so called because they are very precious and give light to people):

I take refuge in the Buddha.   I take refuge in the dharma.   I take refuge in the Sangha.

The Three Jewels are also known as the Three Refuges. A refuge is a place where people are safe from harm. Buddhists find refuge in the example of the Buddha, who found nirvana on his own and discovered the meaning of life. They also find refuge in the dharma, the teachings of the Buddha. The Sangha is the community of monks and nuns who founded monasteries – places of safety where people could go to study and practise Buddhism.

> What makes you noble is if you understand reality, you know if you're a good person. If you're a wise person then you're noble.
> The Buddha

Bhikkhus receiving alms.

> …and good it is to serve the monks…
> The Buddha (in the Dhammapada)

Bhikkhus relaxing outside a temple in Cambodia.

The Five Precepts

All Buddhists are expected to follow the **Five Precepts**, which means observing these rules:

- not to take the life of any living being

- not to take what is not given

- not to take part in sexual misconduct

- not to speak falsely

- not to take drugs that cloud the mind.

From the start, monks also had to follow strict rules that developed from the Eightfold Path. The Sangha was seen as the living representation of the Buddha's teachings and so its members led a strict and disciplined life. As the Sangha grew, so did the number of rules. The only possessions a monk could have were robes to wear, a bowl to collect food in and a razor to shave with.

Bhikkhus meditating in Thailand.

The Sangha today

When Buddhists join the Sangha today, they follow more rules than the **laity**. Once they are full members, there are over two hundred rules to follow, but during their training they have just five rules in addition to the Five Precepts. These are:

- not to eat after midday

- not to sing, dance or play music

- not to wear perfume or jewellery

- not to sit on high chairs or sleep on a soft bed

- not to accept or use money.

The Sangha is highly respected by Buddhists today and some Buddhists believe that only monks can achieve nirvana.

Key vocabulary

bhikkhu A Buddhist monk; nuns are called bhikkhunis

caste system A series of social classes that determine someone's job and status in society

Five Precepts Five rules that all Buddhists are expected to follow

laity Buddhists who are not monks or nuns

Sangha The community of Buddhist monks and nuns

Three Jewels Buddha, dharma, Sangha; also known as the Three Refuges

Check your understanding

1 What is the Sangha?

2 What are the Three Jewels?

3 Why did the Buddha disagree with the caste system?

4 What are the Five Precepts?

5 Explain why members of the Sangha have to live by stricter rules than other Buddhists. Use examples in your answer.

The spread of Buddhism

How did an Indian emperor help Buddhism spread to new lands 200 years after the Buddha's death?

The death of the Buddha

After recruiting followers and establishing the Sangha, the Buddha continued to travel around northern India sharing his teachings. He did this even in old age when his health was failing.

The Buddha's followers were distraught as their leader approached death. However, the Buddha used his final moments to share an important teaching with them: 'He who sees me sees the teaching and he who sees the teaching sees me.' The Buddha did not appoint anyone to succeed him as Buddhist leader. Instead, he told the monks that the dharma would be their guide, and that he would always be there in the dharma.

Following this, the Buddha fell into a meditative trance and finally achieved parinirvana – complete nirvana. Stories tell of how the 'earth quivered like a ship struck by a storm' and beautiful flowers blossomed on the trees above where the Buddha had laid down, showering his body with their petals. The Buddha's body was cremated and the remains divided up and put into eight **stupas**. The stupas became holy sites of **pilgrimage** as Buddhism spread.

> In measured steps the Best of Men walked to this final resting place – no more return in store for him, no further suffering. In full sight of his disciples he lay down on his right side, rested his head on his hand, and put one leg over the other.
>
> A description of the death of the Buddha, from the Pali Canon

The Reclining Buddha in South Korea. It is believed that you can gain good fortune by touching the Buddha's feet.

Fact

Buddhism began in northern India, where people were Hindu. It never became the official religion there, but it was popular for more than 1000 years after the Buddha's death. As Islam expanded into India from the eighth century CE, Buddhism's popularity began to decline, but by this time it had already spread to other parts of the world.

Emperor Ashoka

In the third century BCE, an Indian emperor named Ashoka became the world's first Buddhist ruler. His conversion had a profound impact on the development of Buddhism.

Ashoka ruled over large parts of India. Like his father and grandfather, Ashoka wanted to expand his empire, and he waged many wars to achieve this. In one battle, Ashoka's army captured around 150,000 people and made them slaves; they killed 100,000 more. When Ashoka heard about this bloodthirsty incident he was horrified by the role he had played. He decided that he would no longer follow in the violent footsteps of his father and grandfather. Instead, he would rule his empire according to the Buddhist principles of non-violence and compassion, which he had learned from a Buddhist monk.

Ashoka abandoned his attempts to expand his empire and focused on finding ways to care for the people he already ruled. This involved building hospitals, schools and even digging wells to provide water for thirsty travellers passing through. He also banned the killing of animals. All over his empire, he ordered that pillars and rocks be engraved with words of encouragement for people to behave in a humble, honest and generous way. Although he favoured Buddhism himself, Ashoka insisted that all religions should be tolerated in his empire.

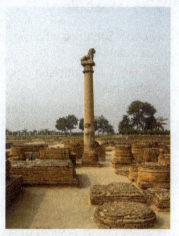

Ashoka built statues around his empire promoting Buddhist virtues.

Buddhism spreads

Ashoka sent **missionaries** to spread the Buddhist message. These missionaries travelled as far as Egypt, Syria and Macedonia. However, they were most successful in Sri Lanka. According to Buddhist tradition, Ashoka even sent his son and daughter as missionaries to Sri Lanka, where they were warmly welcomed by the ruler, King Tissa. Ashoka's daughter took with her a cutting from the Bodhi tree where the Buddha had achieved enlightenment. Although the original tree that grew from this cutting no longer stands, a tree that is believed to be a descendant of it is a popular place of Buddhist pilgrimage today.

In the centuries after the Buddha's death, his teachings were passed on orally. Some were carved into stone by Ashoka, but many were not. Buddhist teachings were first written down by Sri Lankan monks in 29 BCE. They were called the Pali Canon.

Key vocabulary

missionaries People who spread a religious message to different countries

pilgrimage A journey taken to a place of religious importance

stupa A place where the remains of the Buddha were buried

Check your understanding

1 Describe the death of the Buddha.

2 Who was Emperor Ashoka?

3 Explain why Ashoka became a Buddhist.

4 Why is Ashoka such a respected ruler? Give examples.

5 How did Buddhism spread beyond India? Include the word 'missionary' in your answer.

Knowledge organiser

Key vocabulary

ascetic Someone who lives a life of simplicity and self-denial

bhikkhu A Buddhist monk; nuns are called bhikkhunis

Bodh Gaya The holiest site in Buddhism, where Siddhartha meditated under a Bodhi tree and became the Buddha

Brahmins Priests in ancient India who interpreted Queen Maya's dream when she was pregnant with Siddhartha

Buddha The awakened or enlightened one

caste system A series of social classes that determine someone's job and status in society

Dhammapada A Buddhist scripture that contains the teachings and sayings of the Buddha

dharma The Buddha's teachings

dukkha The suffering or dissatisfaction of all living beings

Eightfold Path Eight instructions taught by the Buddha to help people overcome suffering and reach enlightenment

enlightenment The state of being awakened to the truth about life

Five Precepts Five rules that all Buddhists are expected to follow

Four Noble Truths The basis of the Buddha's teachings: all creatures suffer; suffering is caused by selfish desires; suffering can be ended; the way to end suffering is to follow the Eightfold Path

Four Sights Four things seen by Siddhartha when leaving the royal grounds – old age, sickness, death and a holy man

karma The forces that influence people's fortune and future rebirth

laity Buddhists who are not monks or nuns

meditation The practice of focusing the mind

Middle Way A lifestyle between luxury and having nothing at all

missionaries People who spread a religious message to different countries

nirvana A state of bliss experienced by those who have found enlightenment

Pali Canon The main sacred text for many Buddhists which contains the teachings of the Buddha, rules for monks and nuns and the philosophy of Buddhism; also known as the Tipitaka

parable A story used to teach a moral or spiritual lesson

parinirvana A state of complete bliss, entered into by souls that are not reborn

pilgrimage A journey taken to a place of religious importance

samsara The continual process of life, death and rebirth

Sangha The community of Buddhist monks and nuns

Sanskrit An ancient Indian language

scriptures Religious texts

sermon A speech given by a religious leader

stupa A place where the remains of the Buddha were buried

Three Jewels Buddha, dharma, Sangha; also known as the Three Refuges

Three Poisons Greed, hatred and delusion

Key facts

- Buddhism began in India over 2500 years ago. It is now the fourth-largest religion in the world, with approximately 500 million followers. 99% of Buddhists live in Asia. 50% live in China.

- Buddhists believe that everyone is travelling through a cycle of birth, death and rebirth called samsara. A person's actions in this life can affect his or her next one (karma).

- The main sacred text for Buddhists is the Pali Canon, which contains Buddhist philosophy and teachings.

- Buddhism was founded by a prince called Siddhartha Gautama. From childhood, Siddhartha noticed the suffering of other creatures.

- When he was 29 years old, Siddhartha saw four things that changed his view of life: old age, sickness, death and a holy man. He gave up his life of luxury and set out to discover how to end suffering by living as an ascetic.

- Siddhartha eventually realised that denying his body what it needed was as bad as living in luxury. He settled on the Middle Way. Eventually, while sitting under a Bodhi tree, he found enlightenment, nirvana, and became the Buddha.

- The Buddha attracted many followers. They eventually established the Sangha, a community of monks and nuns who dedicate their lives to Buddhism.

- The basis of the Buddha's teachings are the Four Noble Truths: all creatures suffer; suffering is caused by selfish desires; suffering can be ended; the way to end suffering is to follow the Eightfold Path.

- The Eightfold Path is a series of eight steps that Buddhists can follow to help them lead a contented life.

- All Buddhists follow the Five Precepts. Members of the Sangha follow over two hundred more rules, but when they first join there are just five extra rules.

- After the Buddha's death, Buddhism spread to other countries with the help of the Indian Emperor Ashoka, who converted to Buddhism and encouraged it across his large empire.

Key people

Ashoka An Indian emperor who ruled between 272 and 231 BCE and became the first Buddhist ruler

the Buddha The name given to Siddhartha Gautama, an Indian prince born in 563 BCE, after he achieved enlightenment; the central figure of Buddhism

Channa Siddhartha's servant

Devadatta Siddhartha's cousin

Mara The demon Lord who tried to prevent Siddhartha from achieving enlightenment under the Bodhi tree

Maya Siddhartha's mother

Rahula Siddhartha's son

Siddhartha Gautama An Indian prince born in 563 BCE who became the Buddha. He died in 486 BCE

Yashodhara Siddhartha Gautama's cousin and wife

Tian Tan Buddha, also known as the Big Buddha, is a large bronze statue located in Hong Kong. It was completed in 1993.

Buddhism in the modern world

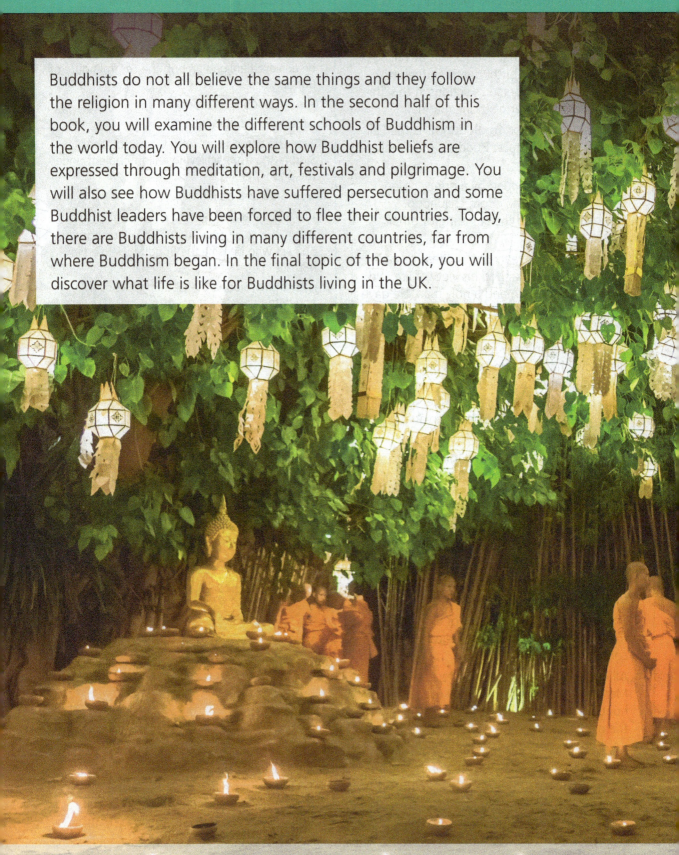

Buddhists do not all believe the same things and they follow the religion in many different ways. In the second half of this book, you will examine the different schools of Buddhism in the world today. You will explore how Buddhist beliefs are expressed through meditation, art, festivals and pilgrimage. You will also see how Buddhists have suffered persecution and some Buddhist leaders have been forced to flee their countries. Today, there are Buddhists living in many different countries, far from where Buddhism began. In the final topic of the book, you will discover what life is like for Buddhists living in the UK.

Unit 2: Buddhism in the modern world
What are the schools of Buddhism?

Buddhism is a diverse religion, with many different branches.
What are the major schools of Buddhism and how do they differ?

In the centuries after the Buddha's death, Buddhism spread rapidly beyond India. As the dharma (Buddha's teaching) reached different countries, a variety of schools, or branches, of Buddhism developed. The two main schools are **Theravada** Buddhism and **Mahayana** Buddhism. Both follow the basic teaching of the Four Noble Truths and the Eightfold Path. They also both promote showing compassion and loving kindness to all living beings. However, there are differences – as there are between followers of many religions – because people have interpreted the Buddha's teachings differently over time. Despite their differences, scholars often highlight how much the various schools of Buddhism also have in common.

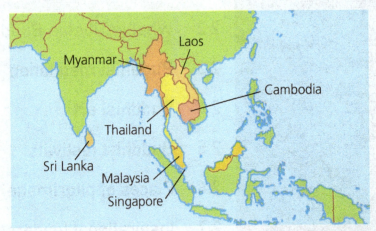

This map shows the countries where Theravada Buddhism is mainly practised.

Theravada Buddhism

Theravada Buddhism can mainly be found in Sri Lanka, Thailand, Myanmar (Burma), Laos and Cambodia. It places special emphasis on the role of the Sangha.

Monks have an important part to play in learning and practising the dharma (see page 60) and mastering meditation. Members of the Sangha are able to concentrate fully on following the dharma because they have left their homes and families behind to live in a monastery. Most Theravada Buddhists accept that it would be impossible for everyone live in this way, but they believe that monks and nuns are more likely than the laity to find nirvana.

> 66 For a vast majority of Buddhists in Theravadin countries, the order of monks is seen by lay Buddhists as a means of gaining the most merit in the hope of accumulating good karma for a better rebirth. 99
> Merv Fowler, *Buddhist Beliefs and Practices* (Sussex Academic Press, 1999), p. 65

Householders

The laity in Theravada Buddhism are often called 'householders'. They support the Sangha in a variety of ways, including making offerings (alms) to the community of monks of food, clothes and even money. Householders are also required to provide the monks with the 'eight requisites'. These are the only personal items that a member of the Sangha is allowed:

- an outer robe
- an inner robe
- a thicker robe for winter
- an alms bowl for gathering food
- a razor
- a needle and thread
- a belt
- a water strainer.

Novice monks with their bowls. These are used to collect food from the laity.

Today, it is not uncommon for monks and nuns to have extra items. These range from simple things like towels, socks or sandals to devices like mobile phones. Whatever they have, it must be shared freely with others, and used for good.

Householders are generous towards the monks because they believe that their presence in the community as teachers and preservers of Buddha's teaching is very important. In return for this support, monks serve the laity by conducting religious rituals such as funerals and by providing instruction in meditation, or schooling. For example, in Thailand, many boys leave home and travel to a nearby monastery to live as a novice monk for a year. As well as learning more about Buddhism, they are taught basic numeracy and literacy, and sometimes even computer skills.

The Tipitaka

Theravada Buddhism is based on a collection of writings called the Pali Canon or the Tipitaka. The Pali Canon is divided into three parts, or 'baskets'. The first basket contains the rules of the Sangha. This community of monks and nuns is very important to Theravadins. The second basket contains the teachings and sayings of the Buddha, including the Dhammapada. The third basket interprets and explains the dharma – the Buddha's teachings.

Mahayana Buddhism

There are many different forms of Mahayana Buddhism, which is most popular in China, Taiwan, Japan, Korea and Tibet. Mahayana Buddhists feel that the term 'Sangha' applies to all Buddhists and that everyone has an equal chance of achieving enlightenment.

While paying special attention to monks and nuns, Mahayana Buddhists also focus on **Bodhisattvas**. A Bodhisattva is someone who has reached enlightenment, but, filled with compassion for the suffering of others, chooses not to enter parinirvana. Instead, he or she is reborn into the world to guide and teach others so that they too can reach enlightenment. There are potentially many thousands of Bodhisattvas. Some are greatly respected by Mahayana Buddhists and are often represented in Buddhist art.

In Mahayana Buddhism the Bodhisattva Avalokitesvara – a Bodhisattva who is believed to have possessed the compassion shown by all Buddhas (those who have achieved nirvana) – is sometimes depicted with 11 faces.

Key vocabulary

Bodhisattva A person who has found enlightenment but is reborn to help others

Mahayana A school of Buddhism that believes in Bodhisattvas and that the term 'Sangha' applies to all Buddhists

Theravada A school of Buddhism that views the Sangha as very important

Check your understanding

1. What are the two major schools of Buddhism and where are they found?
2. Describe what life is like for a monk.
3. Explain why Theravada Buddhism places great emphasis on the Sangha.
4. What role do 'householders' play in Theravada Buddhism? Give examples.
5. How does Mahayana Buddhism differ from Theravada? Give at least two reasons and refer to Bodhisattvas in your answer.

What is Tibetan Buddhism?

Who is the leader of Tibetan Buddhism and how is it practised?

Tibetan Buddhism and Shamanism

Tibet is located in a mountainous area in the Himalayas that borders two vast countries: India to the south and China to the north. Buddhism was brought to Tibet by Indian missionaries in the mid-seventh century CE. Tibetan Buddhism exists within the Mahayana tradition and developed alongside another type of spiritual belief called Shamanism. A shaman is someone who believes he or she can control evil spirits and heal the sick. Traditionally, Buddhism rejects such practices, but their importance to Tibetan culture influenced the way that Buddhism developed there.

This map shows where Mahayana Buddhism is practised. Tibetan Buddhism is found within the Mahayana school.

The Tibetan Book of the Dead

Buddhists believe that all beings are part of the cycle of samsara. Different schools of Buddhism have different ideas about what happens after we die and how we are reborn. Some think that rebirth happens immediately. The Tibetan school teaches that in between death and rebirth people spend time in a state called **bardo**. This is described in the Tibetan Book of the Dead (Bardo Thodol), which explains how after someone dies his or her mind can still experience sights, sounds, smells and tastes. It is this attachment to the senses that causes people to be reborn rather than reach parinirvana.

The book also describes how, after death, people come to stand before Yama, King of the Dead. Yama holds up a mirror, showing them all the actions of their life. Some other religions teach that after death we must face judgement for our actions on earth. However, Tibetan Buddhists do not believe they are judged by Yama – he provides the means for people to judge themselves.

> ❝ The mirror in which Yama seems to read your past is your own memory, and also his judgement is your own. It is you who pronounce your own judgement, which in turn determines your next rebirth. ❞
>
> Tibetan Book of the Dead

Fact

In Tibet, you can often see colourful flags hung from temples and monasteries with prayers and **mantras** written on them. Buddhists believe that the wind carries these words around the world over and over again.

The Tibetan Sangha

In Tibetan Buddhism senior monks are called **lamas**, which means 'teachers'. Monks play an important role in Tibetan society. It is estimated that in the nineteenth century one in six of all men in Tibet were monks and many families expected at least one of their sons to become a monk. Training was intense and took more than 15 years to complete. In most Buddhist countries, monks tended to live away from the world. However, in Tibet, they often worked in trade and politics, and people sometimes asked monks to settle legal disputes. In addition to this, monks spent their time memorising and interpreting sacred texts, practising meditation and maintaining the temples.

Prayer flags near Potala Palace in Tibet, which is where the Dalai Lamas lived until 1959.

The Chinese occupation of Tibet

From the seventeenth century, the **Dalai Lamas** were the spiritual and political leaders of Tibet. This changed in the 1950s, when the Chinese army invaded and occupied Tibet, claiming it was part of China. Fearing capture, the Dalai Lama fled to Dharamsala in India. Many hundreds of monks and other devoted Buddhists followed him on this treacherous journey over the Himalayan mountains into exile. The Dalai Lama still lives in Dharamsala as the head of a Tibetan government and people in exile. Since he left, many Tibetan monasteries have been destroyed or closed down.

Tibetan Buddhists believe that the Dalai Lama is the Bodhisattva Avalokitesvara reborn.

The Dalai Lama

The title Dalai Lama roughly translates as 'ocean of wisdom'. The current Dalai Lama was born as Lhamo Thondup in 1935. Tibetan Buddhists believe he is the fourteenth reincarnation of a Bodhisattva who originally became enlightened in the fourteenth century. The Dalai Lama regularly travels around the world to meet Buddhist and world leaders. He writes books and gives sermons on spiritual issues and communicates with his followers through social media and the internet.

Key vocabulary

bardo A state of being that exists between death and rebirth

Dalai Lama The leader of Tibetan Buddhism, believed to be an incarnation of the Bodhisattva Avalokitesvara

lama A senior monk or teacher in Tibetan Buddhism

mantra A sacred phrase that is chanted during meditation

Check your understanding

1 When did Buddhism reach Tibet?

2 What is Shamanism?

3 Explain Tibetan Buddhist teachings about rebirth. Include a quotation from the Tibetan Book of the Dead in your answer.

4 Why does the current Dalai Lama live in India and not Tibet?

5 Why is the Dalai Lama an important religious leader? Give examples to support your points.

Buddhist meditation

Meditation is important in all schools of Buddhism, but how do Buddhists practise it?

How to meditate

The Buddha taught his followers that if they trained and controlled their minds through meditation they could reach nirvana. Some of the Buddha's teachings on meditation can be found in chapter 3 of the Dhammapada. In this chapter, the Buddha likens the training of the mind to an archer: 'Just as an archer straightens an arrow, so the discerning man straightens his mind — so fickle and unsteady, so difficult to guard.'

In order to meditate, a Buddhist will find a quiet place where he or she can sit comfortably. Many will choose to sit cross-legged on the floor with their back straight and their arms lightly resting upon their knees or in their lap. This is known as the **lotus** position.

The lotus is a symbol of the states of mind taught about by the Buddha.

The lotus flower

The lotus flower is an important symbol in Buddhism and it is often seen to represent the states of mind that the Buddha taught about. The flower grows in muddy water, which represents the cloudy or troubled mind that is unenlightened. However, the lotus flower blossoms above the water, and this represents the mind reaching enlightenment.

Fact

Buddhists may meditate in front of statues of the Buddha, but this is not the same as praying to him or worshipping him as a god. The word 'worship' means to show worth to someone or something. In this sense, Buddhists can be said to take part in worship as they show respect to the life and teachings of the Buddha.

Once in position, their meditation begins with simply being still and aware of themselves. Meditators usually close their eyes and focus their mind. They do this by concentrating on their breathing and then bringing it under control in a regular and calm pattern. Sometimes Buddhists will concentrate on an object when meditating. This might be a statue of the Buddha or a Bodhisattva, a candle or a flower. Some Buddhists also choose to focus on a skeleton or corpse, as it encourages them to realise the truth that life is not permanent.

Many Buddhists meditate in silence, but often senior monks will lead guided meditation in which they talk while followers listen to the words of their leader. In some Buddhist schools, mantras and passages of scripture such as the Three Refuges are repeatedly chanted.

The jhanas

The word **jhana** means 'state of absorption'. In the Eightfold Path, it is sometimes translated as 'right concentration'. The Buddha taught that there are different stages of meditation and that in each stage the meditator becomes more and more absorbed. The jhanas are broken down into the following stages:

1. pleasant feelings
2. joy
3. contentment
4. peace
5. moving beyond the senses into the infinity of time and space
6. exploring the infinity of the mind
7. nothingness
8. neither perception nor non-perception.

The Buddha is often depicted in the lotus position.

The last four stages of the jhanas are difficult to describe. Buddhists believe that it takes years of training to reach them. Even those who are very close to finding enlightenment often struggle to describe what they have experienced. Many Buddhists believe that the only way to understand meditation fully is to do it yourself.

> 66 Better to live one day wise in meditation than to live a hundred years as a fool. 99
>
> Dhammapada chapter 8, verse 111

Meditation can be done anywhere, but different schools of Buddhism sometimes favour different locations. For example, in Theravada Buddhism, some monks often choose to meditate in a forest. Many Buddhists will visit a temple or monastery on holy days to meditate in front of a statue of the Buddha.

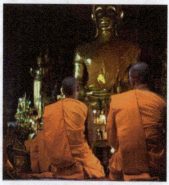
Buddhist monks meditating in front of statue of the Buddha in Laos.

Key vocabulary

jhana A state of absorption – a stage on the path to nirvana through meditation

lotus A flower and key symbol in Buddhism; also used to describe a position used in meditation

Activity

Write a guide to meditation for a Buddhist wanting to find out more about it.

Check your understanding

1 What is meditation?
2 Why might some people say that meditation is not worship?
3 Describe how a Buddhist might practise meditation.
4 Describe how the lotus symbol helps explain the importance of meditation to Buddhists.
5 Describe the jhanas and why some people might struggle to explain them.

Buddhist art

How do Buddhists express their beliefs through art, such as statues, sculptures and mandalas?

Early Buddhists carved scenes from the life of the Buddha into stone and on to cave walls. They believed that it would be disrespectful to show the Buddha as a human, so he is often represented by an empty seat in early Buddhist art. His teachings are often symbolised by a wheel, footprints containing lotus flowers or a royal umbrella or parasol.

Greek stone carvers working in India in the second century CE were the first people to portray the Buddha in human form. Their statues were made to decorate temples and monasteries, but they were also created to teach people who couldn't read Buddhist scriptures about the life and teachings of the Buddha.

The Giant Buddha statue in China is 71 metres tall. It is carved into a mountainside and shows him with long earlobes.

Representations of the Buddha

Statues show the Buddha in different poses each having an important symbolic meaning. Some show the Buddha as starving, which reminds Buddhists that Siddhartha did not find enlightenment through asceticism.

Many statues show him with extremely long earlobes. This may be a reference to Siddhartha's life of luxury as a prince. Wealthy people wore jewellery such as heavy earrings filled with precious stones. These stretched the earlobes, so in early Indian society long earlobes suggested royalty and riches. Statues of the Buddha with elongated earlobes symbolise the Buddhist teaching of the Middle Way and the rejection of luxury. They can also symbolise his compassion and ability to listen.

One of the most famous depictions of the Buddha shows him lying down, or reclining. This reminds Buddhists of the Buddha's death and entry into parinirvana.

Although the Buddha taught people to reject wealth, rich kings and rulers of Buddhist countries have often used expensive materials when creating Buddhist art. One of the most famous examples of this is the Golden Buddha statue in Bangkok, Thailand. The statue is about 700 years old and is made of solid gold. It shows that Buddhists wanted to portray Buddha as an important person, even if such expense conflicts with the teaching of the Middle Way.

There are many other images and symbols of the Buddha. Some show him sitting with his right hand up, the palm facing outwards. This signifies a shield and shows that the Buddha offers protection from suffering. Other statues depict him walking, which signifies the journeys he took to find enlightenment and then to preach the dharma.

The Golden Buddha in Bangkok is worth an estimated £200 million.

Mandalas

Tibetan Buddhism is the school of Buddhism most associated with **mandalas**. Each part of a mandala has a symbolic meaning. In the centre there is usually either a figure (such as the Buddha or Bodhisavattas) or a shape representing a key part of Buddhism (such as compassion, dukkha or wisdom). Around this are four doors through which you can reach the centre. The colours also symbolise important Buddhist ideas. Blue represents the truth of the dharma, white stands for purity and red signifies compassion.

2.4

Activity

Draw three different representations of the Buddha and label them to explain what each one means.

The image of the bhavacakra can be found on the walls of most monasteries and and temples in Tibet.

The most famous Tibetan mandala is the **bhavacakra**, or wheel of life. The being holding the wheel is thought to be Yama, the King of the Dead. The main divisions on the wheel represent the realms into which people can be reborn, including as an animal or a ghost. In the centre are three animals chasing each other in a circle. These represent the Three Poisons of greed, hatred and delusion. In the top right, the Buddha stands outside the wheel, showing that he has achieved nirvana and escaped the cycle of samsara.

Key vocabulary

bhavacakra a particular Tibetan Buddhist mandala depicting the cycle of samsara

mandala A circular pattern that has symbolic meanings and is used to help people meditate

Making a mandala

Tibetan monks are also famous for constructing beautiful and intricate mandalas using coloured sand. It can take days, weeks or even months to complete, and the monks use special tools to ensure that each grain of sand falls into exactly the right place. These mandalas are displayed during Buddhist festivals. After the festival, the sand is often brushed and mixed together before being collected and poured into a nearby river or stream. This act is also symbolic, demonstrating the Buddhist belief that everything is impermanent.

Check your understanding

1 How did early Buddhist art depict the Buddha?

2 Explain two symbolic ways that the Buddha is represented.

3 What is the bhavacakra?

4 Explain the meaning of the bhavacakra.

5 Explain why Tibetan monks destroy mandalas after they have made them.

Unit 2: Buddhism in the modern world
Buddhist festivals

Festivals are held to mark important events in the life
of the Buddha. Who takes part in these festivals and
what happens?

Wesak

Wesak is the most important festival for many
Buddhists. In Western countries it is often called
'Buddha Day'. The festival is a time to remember the
Buddha's birth, his enlightenment (nirvana) and his
death (parinirvana). There is no fixed date for Wesak
and it is celebrated at different times in different
countries. In most Asian countries, it happens on
the first full moon in May. This is because Theravada
Buddhists believe that all three events in the Buddha's
life took place under a full moon.

Water being poured over a statue of the Buddha during
the festival of Wesak.

In countries where Buddhism is the main religion,
Wesak is usually a public holiday. Early in the morning,
Buddhists visit their nearest temple or monastery,
where monks give talks and lead the chanting of
mantras, including the Three Jewels. The laity bring gifts of flowers,
rice, candles and incense, which are placed by statues or shrines of the
Buddha. Some Buddhists also pour water over a statue of the Buddha.
This symbolises the washing away of one's past misdeeds and the dousing
of the Three Poisons (greed, hatred and delusion).

During Wesak, some Buddhists remind themselves of the importance of
the Five Precepts, and others will adopt some extra precepts on the day,
such as not eating after midday and not wearing perfume or jewellery.
Many Buddhists will mark the occasion by donating to charity or giving
free food and drink to those in need.

Vassa

In Theravada Buddhism, the period of **Vassa** lasts for the three months
of the Asian rainy season. Monks stay in their monasteries and avoid any
travel. It is known as the 'rains retreat' because monks retreat into their
monasteries. This tradition dates back to the time of the Buddha and the
first Sangha, who stayed in one place as it was too difficult to travel on
foot to spread their teachings during this time. During Vassa, monks will
practise even more intensive meditation than usual. The laity might choose
to give up things like meat and alcohol. This has led some in the West to
refer to Vassa as 'Buddhist Lent', although many Christians and Buddhists
reject this comparison.

Kathina

Within one month of Vassa ending, the festival of **Kathina** takes place. This is when Buddhists show gratitude to the monks for the end of the rainy season. The origins of Kathina are linked to a legend from the life of the Buddha. According to the legend, a group of 30 monks were travelling to spend the 'rains retreat' with the Buddha. However, the rainy season began before they had finished their journey, so the monks had to stay where they were for three months. After this, they went to see the Buddha. To reward them, the Buddha gave them some cloth and told the travelling monks to turn it into a robe. The Buddha said that they should then decide which of them deserved it. By doing this, the Buddha enforced the idea that monks are not allowed possessions and even their robes must be donated. The story also encourages monks to be self-sufficient by making their own clothes and to show generosity by giving clothes to each other.

During the festival of Kathina, monks are often given gifts of money and cloth.

Gifts to the monks

In some Theravada countries, the laity commemorate this story by taking cloth to monks during Kathina. Usually, one or two monks will accept the cloth on behalf of the rest. The Sangha then spend the day cutting the cloth and fashioning it into robes before deciding which monk will receive the gift. As well as cloth, food, basic sanitary supplies and money are sometimes given to the Sangha. These gifts sustain the monks over the coming year. They are freely given to the monks as a way of saying thank you for the work they do to support the community.

Key vocabulary

Kathina A festival of gratitude to the Sangha

Vassa The period of the rainy season, when monks stay in their monasteries

Wesak A festival to commemorate the Buddha's birth, enlightenment and death; also known as Buddha Day

Check your understanding

1 What three events in the Buddha's life are celebrated at Wesak?
2 When is Wesak celebrated?
3 Explain why some Buddhists mark Wesak by pouring water over a statue of the Buddha.
4 What story from the life of the Buddha is remembered at Kathina?
5 How do the laity show gratitude to the Sangha at Kathina?

Unit 2: Buddhism in the modern world
Places of pilgrimage

What are the main sites of Buddhist pilgrimage and why do Buddhists visit these places?

Just before the Buddha died, he told his followers to remember him by going on pilgrimage to four holy places. These are the sites of his birth, his enlightenment, his first teaching and his death. At all these sites, temples and shrines containing relics of the Buddha have been built. By visiting these places, Buddhists can reflect on the events of the Buddha's life and may feel a stronger connection to him. However, there is no obligation for Buddhists to go on pilgrimage, and many Buddhists never visit pilgrimage sites.

This map shows the locations of the four main sites of Buddhist pilgrimage.

Lumbini

The Buddha's birthplace, Lumbini, is in the foothills of the Himalayas in Nepal. Emperor Ashoka visited Lumbini in the third century BCE. He ordered for the site to be marked with a stone pillar on which was carved 'Here the Buddha was born'. Lumbini was deserted for a long time, but in 1896 a German explorer rediscovered Ashoka's pillar. Since then, the area has remained a place of interest for archaeologists, who try to learn more about the history of Buddhism by studying the remains of buildings and other ancient objects. In recent years, both Theravada and Tibetan monasteries have been established in Lumbini.

A stone marking the site of the Buddha's birth in Lumbini, Nepal.

> 66 Millions of people get immense inspiration. Buddha's spirit always there. But real Buddha's holy places is in one's self. That's important. So real Buddha's sacred place must build within ourselves. We must build within our heart. 99
>
> The Dalai Lama on the significance of pilgrimage for Buddhists

Bodh Gaya

The most important place in the world for Buddhists is Bodh Gaya, where the Buddha achieved enlightenment. Every year, hundreds of thousands of people visit from all over the world. The main attraction is the Mahabodhi Temple, which is believed to have been built by Emperor Ashoka. At the back of the temple, there is a Bodhi tree. According to legend, the tree is a descendant of the Bodhi tree under which the Buddha found enlightenment. It can be crowded near the tree, but pilgrims often meditate around it, believing that this will help them in their own search for enlightenment. There is also a statue in Bodh Gaya called the Great Buddha. It is 25 metres high and was completed in 1989 after seven years of building by over 12,000 bricklayers.

The Mahabodhi Temple in Bodh Gaya.

Sarnath

On the site of the deer park at Sarnath where the Buddha gave his first sermon stands the Dhamekh Stupa. Pilgrims walk around the Dhamekh Stupa three times, one for each of the Three Jewels. The circle also symbolises the cycle of samsara. Sarnath was a vibrant Buddhist area until it was destroyed in the twelfth century CE by Muslim conquerors. The area was rediscovered in 1937 and is now a thriving Buddhist community again, with many monasteries that pilgrims visit.

The Dhamekh Stupa in Sarnath.

Kusinara

At the site of the Buddha's parinirvana is the Mahaparinirvana Temple and Stupa, which are said to be built on the exact spot that the Buddha died. The ruins of several monasteries can also be found in this area. Buddhist pilgrims also visit the nearby Ramabhar Stupa, where the Buddha was cremated.

Other sites of pilgrimage

The four sites specifically mentioned by the Buddha are usually considered to be the most important, but there are several other sites of Buddhist pilgrimage across Asia. Many people believe that these sites contain relics of the Buddha, including his hair and teeth. These objects prove to Buddhists that the Buddha really existed, and they are a way of connecting with his life and teachings. At some sites there are also ancient monasteries.

Activity

Imagine you have been on a Buddhist pilgrimage to a destination of your choice. Write a diary account of your experience.

Check your understanding

1. What four sites did the Buddha tell his followers they should visit after his death?
2. Which of the four sites is the most important? Explain why this is.
3. Why might Buddhist pilgrims walk around the Dhamekh Stupa three times?
4. What are relics and why are they kept?
5. 'All Buddhists should go on pilgrimage.' Discuss this statement.

Unit 2: Buddhism in the modern world
Inspirational leaders

How have inspiring Buddhist leaders helped spread the religion around the world?

Maha Ghosananda

Maha Ghosananda was born into a family of farmers in Cambodia in 1929 and became a novice Theravada monk at the age of 14. He continued his education and training at universities in Cambodia, where he studied under some of the most respected Buddhist masters of his time. Ghosananda travelled and studied in both India and Thailand. While he was living as a monk in Thailand, tragedy unfolded in his homeland.

In 1975, Cambodia was taken over by a group called the Khmer Rouge, led by the dictator Pol Pot. The Khmer Rouge evacuated the cities and sent the people on forced marches to work on special projects in the countryside. In Cambodia, 1975 became year 0, and the Khmer Rouge attempted to rebuild the country's economy based on basic farming. They discarded Western medicine and tried to rid the country of Buddhism by destroying temples, monasteries and libraries. Doctors, teachers, monks, those who spoke a foreign language and anyone who wore glasses were executed.

Ghosananda refused to stand by and do nothing while such terrible things were happening in his country. He left his community in Thailand and worked in refugee camps along the Thailand–Cambodia border. The people he encountered had fled the Khmer Rouge through hazardous jungle. They were so starved of food that Ghosananda described them as walking skeletons. In the refugee camps he built basic Buddhist temples and organised classes where people discussed the Buddha's teachings on forgiveness and compassion.

By the time the Khmer Rouge regime collapsed in 1979, nearly every Buddhist monastery and temple in Cambodia had been destroyed. The Sangha had nearly been wiped out. Prior to 1975, there had been approximately 70,000 monks; in 1979, there were fewer than 3000. Those who had not been murdered were either living secretly among the laity or had fled to other countries. Nearly all of Maha Ghosananda's family and friends were dead.

When Ghosananda returned to Cambodia, he re-established the Sangha. He made contact with monks who had gone into hiding or fled overseas and organised the rebuilding of temples. He became particularly famous for leading an annual 125-mile 'peace walk'. He devoted the rest of his

Cambodia is in Southeast Asia and borders Thailand, Vietnam and Laos.

Fact

Under Pol Pot's regime, it is estimated that at least two million Cambodians, out of a total population of eight million, died from torture, executions, overwork, starvation and disease.

The site in Cambodia known as 'The Killing Fields' where over 8900 people were murdered.

life to encouraging people of different religions to talk to one another and try to understand and respect one another's beliefs. He also campaigned for non-violent solutions to conflict. He was nominated four times for the Nobel Peace Prize. Maha Ghosananda died in 2007.

Maha Ghosananda is sometimes referred to as the 'Gandhi of Cambodia'.

> 66 Cambodia has suffered deeply.
> From deep suffering comes deep compassion.
> From deep compassion comes a peaceful heart.
> From a peaceful heart comes a peaceful person.
> From a peaceful person comes a peaceful family and community.
> From peaceful communities comes a peaceful nation.
> From peaceful nations come a peaceful world. 99
>
> A poem by Maha Ghosananda in his book *Step by Step* (Parallax Press, 1992)

Thich Nhat Hanh

Thich Nhat Hanh was born in Vietnam in 1926 and became a Buddhist monk at the age of 16. During the Vietnam War, fought between North and South Vietnam, Nhat Hanh called for peace. He also founded an order of monks who made it their mission to help victims of the war. Surrounded by violence, this was often dangerous work.

During the Vietnam War, the USA sent soldiers to support South Vietnam. In 1966, Nhat Hanh travelled to the USA to give speeches against the war, calling for a non-violent solution to the conflict. As a result, Vietnamese leaders banned him from returning to Vietnam. The following year, Nhat Hanh was nominated for the Nobel Peace Prize by Martin Luther King, who greatly admired his intellect and calls for peace.

Today, Nhat Hanh campaigns for peace and social justice from a Buddhist centre he set up in southern France called Plum Village. Many monks, nuns and laity live there and they welcome thousands of visitors a year. The community also interacts with Buddhists around the world via social media. Nhat Hanh was finally allowed to visit his homeland again in 2005.

Thich Nhat Hanh remains a popular teacher of meditation and is the author of over 100 books.

Check your understanding

1 Where is Cambodia?

2 What happened in Cambodia between 1975 and 1979?

3 Explain how Maha Ghosananda helped to re-establish Buddhism in Cambodia.

4 Explain what Maha Ghosananda meant in the quote on this page.

5 Why was Thich Nhat Hanh nominated for the Nobel Peace Prize?

Buddhism in the UK

How did Buddhism become established in the UK and how do British Buddhists practise their religion?

History

Today Buddhism is a growing religion in Britain, but for most of the religion's history, it has had no British followers. British people first began taking an interest in Buddhism in the late 1800s, when government workers were sent to work overseas in Buddhist countries. Some of these workers translated Buddhist texts such as the Pali Canon into English. In 1924, a British lawyer set up an organisation called the Buddhist Society in London. Today, the society runs courses and hosts lectures on many different forms of Buddhism. It also has a library containing important Buddhist texts.

After the Chinese invasion of Tibet in 1950, many Tibetan Buddhists came to Britain. The religion's popularity in Britain also grew throughout the 1960s, as people began to travel abroad more often. Many Buddhists living in Britain today have converted to Buddhism from another religion or belief system.

> 66 I can give my teachings in brief. I can teach in detail. It is those who understand that are hard to find. 99
>
> The Buddha

> **Fact**
>
> Over the last 100 years, the UK's Buddhist population has grown to over 200,000 people.

Chithurst

One of the largest Buddhist centres in the UK is in Chithurst, Sussex. The centre's Buddhist name is Cittaviveka, which means 'withdrawn mind'. It is one of five Theravada monasteries in the UK. Cittaviveka was founded in 1979 by a Thai monk. The monastery places an emphasis on following the Five Precepts and other monastic rules while living in a community.

The monastery is part of what is known as the **Thai Forest Tradition**. As such, it has large grounds, mostly made up of woodland containing huts where monks and nuns can retreat and meditate in complete silence and solitude. There are also two houses, one for men and one for women. Men and women tend to stay separate from each other as part of the monastic rules. These houses are used for eating, teaching and accommodating guests who visit the monastery. The monks and nuns live under strict rules. For example, they are forbidden from accepting or even handling money. Like monks in Thailand and Cambodia, a few members of the community go to the local towns and villages to gather donations of food. The community relies heavily on local Buddhists and friends of the monastery for their food and other supplies.

A Sri Lankan Buddhist at Chithurst monastery.

Samye Ling

Samye Ling monastery in southeast Scotland was the first Tibetan Buddhist centre in the West. It was founded in the late 1960s by Tibetan monks who had fled the Chinese invasion of their homeland. Today, it is home to 60 Buddhists.

Those wishing to become monks train themselves in meditation at the monastery for a minimum of 10 years. They learn Tibetan dharma, language and medicine. The monastery is also popular with tourists, who can have guided tours and take part in meditation classes and courses, which can last for a day or over a week. Samye Ling has become well known for creating and restoring **thangkas**. These are Tibetan Buddhist paintings, on cotton or silk, of the Buddha, a Bodhisattva or a mandala.

A statue of the face of the Buddha in the roots of a tree. Many Buddhists feel closest to the dharma in nature.

Rokpa

Buddhists at Samye Ling try to help the wider community. In 1980, the head monk started the Rokpa charity. *Rokpa* is a Tibetan word meaning to help or serve. The charity helps the poorest people in Nepal, especially children. After the 2015 earthquake in Nepal, Rokpa gave emergency supplies and shelter to victims of the disaster.

Buddhism in the UK is diverse, both in terms of how it is followed and where it is located. The rise of the internet and social media means that anyone who is curious can find out about Buddhism and seek guidance on the dharma and meditation. Buddhism has grown into a variety of traditions as it has spread across the world. It is a living faith with a strong message of compassion, personal reflection and understanding. People are still learning and trying to understand the original teachings of the Buddha, 2500 years after his death.

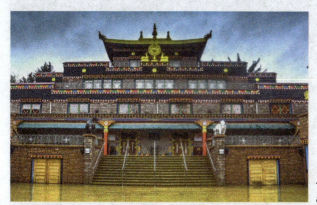

The main temple building at Samye Ling.

Key vocabulary

Thai Forest Tradition A form of Theravada Buddhism that encourages monks and nuns to retreat into the forest to practise meditation in complete solitude

thangkas A Tibetan Buddhist painting on to cotton or silk

Check your understanding

1 How did interest in Buddhism begin in Britain?
2 What is the Buddhist Society and what does it do?
3 Describe the workings of the Buddhist monastery at Chithurst.
4 How did Tibetan Buddhism come to Scotland?
5 Explain the practical work of the Samye Ling community in putting Buddhist beliefs into practice.

Unit 2: Buddhism in the modern world
Knowledge organiser

Key vocabulary

bardo A state of being that exists between death and rebirth

bhavacakra A particular Tibetan Buddhist mandala depicting the cycle of samsara

Bodhisattva A person who has found enlightenment but is reborn to help others

Dalai Lama The leader of Tibetan Buddhism, believed to be an incarnation of the Bodhisattva Avalokitesvara

jhana A state of absorption – a stage on the path to nirvana through meditation

Kathina A festival of gratitude to the Sangha

lama A senior monk or teacher in Tibetan Buddhism

lotus A flower and key symbol in Buddhism; also used to describe a position used in meditation

Mahayana A school of Buddhism that believes in Bodhisattvas and that the term 'Sangha' applies to all Buddhists

mandala A circular pattern that has symbolic meanings and is used to help people meditate

mantra A sacred phrase that is chanted during meditation

Thai Forest Tradition A form of Theravada Buddhism that encourages monks and nuns to retreat into the forest to practise meditation in complete solitude

thangkas A Tibetan Buddhist painting on cotton or silk

Theravada A school of Buddhism that views the Sangha as very important

Vassa The period of the rainy season, when monks stay in their monasteries

Wesak A festival to commemorate the Buddha's birth, enlightenment and death; also known as Buddha Day

Golden statue of Guanyin, a female bodhisattva who embodies the compassion of all Buddhas, at Lushan Temple, China.

Key facts

- Two of the main schools of Buddhism are Theravada and Mahayana. They share many similarities, but Theravada Buddhists place greater emphasis on the Sangha.

- The third main school of Buddhism is Tibetan Buddhism. Tibetan Buddhists have slightly different beliefs, including the belief that between death and rebirth people spend time in a state called bardo.

- The leader of Tibetan Buddhism is the Dalai Lama, who was forced into exile after China invaded Tibet in the 1950s.

- Meditation is a key practice of Buddhists. This involves being still and focusing the mind.

- Buddhists honour the Buddha in art such as huge statues and sculptures and symbolic images such as mandalas.

- The key Buddhist festivals are Wesak (marking the Buddha's birth, enlightenment and death), Vassa (when monks remain in their monasteries during the rainy season) and Kathina (when people celebrate the end of the rainy season by bringing gifts to the monks).

- There are four main sites of Buddhist pilgrimage: Lumbini, Bodh Gaya, Sarnath and Kusinara. These are where Siddhartha was born, enlightened, and as the Buddha taught his first sermon and entered parinirvana.

- The spread of Buddhism in the twentieth century was helped by several inspiring leaders including Maha Ghosananda and Thich Nhat Hanh.

- There are more than 200,000 Buddhists in the UK today. Significant places include the Chithurst and Samye Ling monasteries.

The Golden Wheel of Dharma and Deer sculpture, The Jokhang Temple (most sacred temple in Tibet).

The Dalai Lama is the spiritual leader of the Tibetan people.

Key people

Dalai Lama The spiritual leader of Tibetan Buddhism

Maha Ghosananda A senior monk in Cambodia who helped rebuild the country after war

Thich Nhat Hanh A famous Vietnamese monk who now lives in France

Sikhism

History and belief

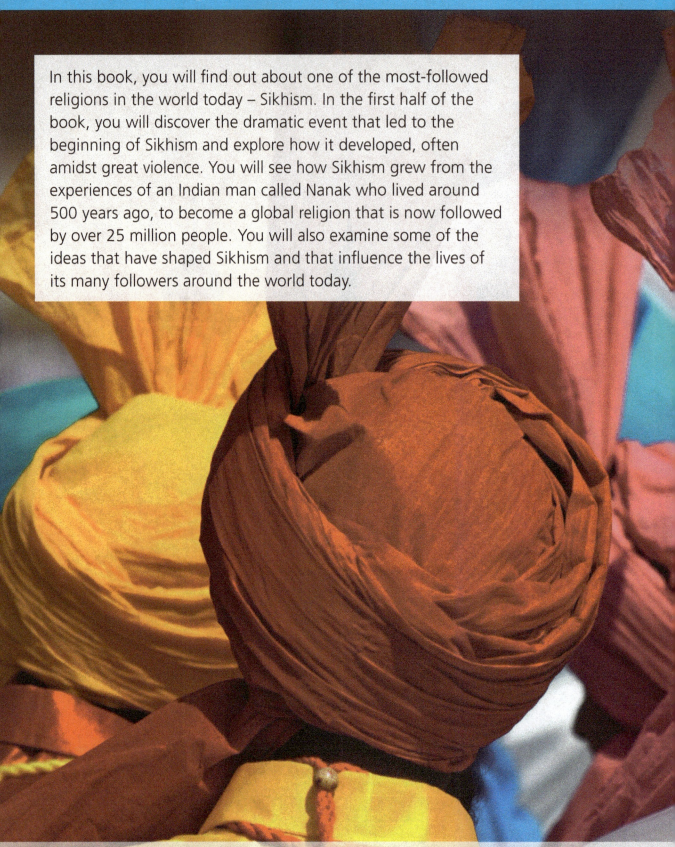

In this book, you will find out about one of the most-followed religions in the world today – Sikhism. In the first half of the book, you will discover the dramatic event that led to the beginning of Sikhism and explore how it developed, often amidst great violence. You will see how Sikhism grew from the experiences of an Indian man called Nanak who lived around 500 years ago, to become a global religion that is now followed by over 25 million people. You will also examine some of the ideas that have shaped Sikhism and that influence the lives of its many followers around the world today.

How did Sikhism begin?

Sikhism began in India nearly 550 years ago. Today, it has approximately 25 million followers, known as Sikhs, but how did the religion begin?

Number	Country	Sikhs
1	India	19,000,000
2	UK	707,000
3	USA	500,300
4	Canada	405,000
5	Malaysia	100,000
6	Australia	72,000
7	Italy	71,000
8	Thailand	70,000
9	Pakistan	50,000
10	Philippines	3,000

This table shows the 10 countries in the world with the highest Sikh populations.

Nanak's childhood

The roots of Sikhism date back to a man named Nanak. He was born in 1469 CE into a Hindu family and grew up in an area of India called Punjab. In 1947, Punjab was split between India, which was mostly Sikh and Hindu, and Pakistan, which was mostly Muslim. The village where Nanak was born is now known as Nankana Sahib and lies near Lahore in present-day Pakistan.

After Nanak's death, several stories were written about his childhood in a book called the **Janam Sakhis.** Many of these stories involve miraculous events. For example, one of them tells how one day Nanak's father asked him to look after his cows. While doing so, Nanak began to meditate, allowing the cows to escape into a neighbour's field. The neighbour was furious, but when he went to inspect the field he discovered no damage at all. The cows had left no footprints and had not eaten a single blade of grass.

Another story tells of how Nanak once fell into a trance while thinking about God. A dangerous snake called a hooded cobra slid alongside him, but instead of attacking Nanak the cobra shielded him from the sun. No one can say for sure whether these stories are accounts of real events, but they show that the early Sikhs who wrote them down regarded Nanak as a very special person.

> ### Fact
> The vast majority of **Sikhs** live in India, which is where the religion began. However, Sikhism has also spread to other countries, including the UK, which is now home to more than 700,000 Sikhs.

This map shows the region of India, Pakistan and Bangladesh.

The story of the hooded cobra is one of many that suggest how important early Sikhs thought Nanak was.

The Mughal Empire

In the sixteenth and seventeenth centuries, most of India was part of the **Mughal Empire**. The Mughals were Muslim conquerors from the area that is now Afghanistan. Many Mughal emperors promoted religious tolerance, but some were cruel. Hindus did not like being ruled over by Muslims and were often persecuted by them. Many battles were fought between the Mughals and the Sikhs. In Sikh scripture, Nanak is quoted as saying:

The Kings are butchers and cruelty is their knife. Their sense of duty has taken wings and flown. (Guru Granth Sahib 145:10)

The Janam Sakhis portray Nanak as an extremely clever child who loved to challenge the religious beliefs and practices of his family and society. Although Nanak was born into a Hindu family, he probably came across other religions at an early age. He would have been particularly aware of Islam, because his father worked as an accountant for the local Muslim authorities.

Nanak's disappearance in the river

According to Sikh tradition, when Nanak was about 30 years old, he had an experience that changed his life. Early one morning he went to the Kali Bein river to wash and pray. He left his clothes on the bank and waded into the water – and then he vanished. When Nanak did not return, his family and friends feared that he had drowned. They dredged the river with nets and searched along the banks, but Nanak was nowhere to be seen.

Three days later, Nanak reappeared, but he was in a trance and did not speak for a long time. When he did speak, he explained that he had been with God, and had been given a special revelation. Nanak proclaimed: '[There is] no Hindu nor Muslim, but only man. So whose path shall I follow? I shall follow God's path. God is neither Hindu nor Muslim and the path which I follow is God's.'

The meaning of this message was that while there are many different religions – which are often in conflict – there is only one God. Sikhs are therefore **monotheists** and believe that God loves all people equally, no matter how they worship him. This revelation also taught people the importance of religious equality and freedom. From this moment on, Nanak was given the title **Guru,** meaning a religious teacher or guide. Nanak was the first of 10 Sikh Gurus.

Key vocabulary

Guru A religious teacher or guide who leads a follower from spiritual ignorance ('gu', 'darkness') into spiritual enlightenment ('ru', 'light')

Janam Sakhis Stories about the childhood and life of Guru Nanak

monotheist Someone who believes in only one God

Mughal Empire The rulers of the area that is now India and Pakistan in the sixteenth and seventeenth centuries

revelation A message revealed by God to humans

Sikh A follower of Sikhism; the name comes from the Sanskrit word shishya, which means 'disciple' or 'learner'

Check your understanding

1 How many Sikhs are there in the world and where do they live?
2 When and where did Sikhism begin?
3 What was the Mughal Empire?
4 Describe what happened when Nanak was 30 years old.
5 Why is the early life of Guru Nanak important to Sikhs? Give examples to support your points.

How did Nanak spread his message?

What did Nanak do after his dramatic encounter with God?

Guru Nanak's encounter with God affected him deeply. He was convinced that it was his duty to share the revelation he had received. Over a period of twenty years, Nanak went on four long journeys. He visited holy Buddhist and Hindu sites as well as the Muslim cities of Mecca and Medina in Arabia. On all his spiritual journeys, he spoke to and debated with religious people. For example, when in Medina, he told Muslims that it made no sense to pray facing towards Mecca because God is everywhere.

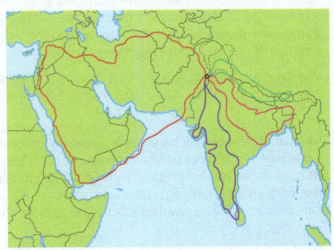

This map shows the journeys Guru Nanak took to spread the word of his revelation.

The miracle of blood and milk

During the first of his journeys, Guru Nanak performed a miracle. A man called Lalo heard that Nanak was passing his house. He ran out to meet him and insisted that the Guru stay and eat with him. Lalo was a hard-working carpenter, but he was of a low **caste** and did not have much money. This meant he was only able to provide Nanak with basic food, but he was very generous with what he had.

In the same village lived a rich but cruel and corrupt man called Malik Bhago. When Malik heard that the Guru was staying with a poor carpenter, he invited Nanak to join him for a luxurious feast. Nanak took Lalo with him to the wealthy man's house, but refused to eat anything. Instead, he sat meditating quietly. Annoyed by the Guru's actions, Malik said: 'You are dishonouring my high caste by eating dry **chapatis** in the house of a low-caste carpenter. I am offering you delicious food. Why do you refuse to eat it?'

Nanak took a chapati from Lalo in one hand and a chapati from Malik in the other. As he squeezed them, milk flowed out from Lalo's, but blood dripped from Malik's. The people at the feast were shocked. Malik demanded to know what this insult meant. Guru Nanak told Malik that he had gained his food by treating people as slaves and causing suffering, whereas Lalo had earned his food through hard, honest work. 'The wealth gathered by cruelty towards the poor is like draining their blood,' Nanak explained. 'Malik Bhago, you invited me to drink blood, leaving the food that is as pure as milk. How could I accept it?' This story emphasises one of Guru Nanak's core teachings: kirat karna (honest labour).

Lalo became one of the earliest followers of Sikhism. He is known today as **Bhai** Lalo. Bhai means 'brother' and is a title that Sikhs give to those they respect.

Activity

Imagine you were at the feast at Malik's house. Write a diary entry describing the events of the evening. Explain how people reacted and what you think Nanak was trying to show.

Guru Nanak went on a number of journeys to spread the revelation he received from God.

The establishment of Kartarpur

After spending 20 years travelling, Guru Nanak and the **disciples** he had gathered on his journeys set up the first permanent Sikh community at a place called **Kartarpur**, meaning the city or seat of God. Every day, Nanak's followers prayed and did community work. They cooked food and welcomed anyone who wished to eat with them, regardless of their caste or religion.

Nanak is highly respected by Sikhs but he is not worshiped as a God.

The death of Guru Nanak

Nanak died on 22 September 1539, at the age of 70. Because the disciples at Kartarpur had been both Muslims and Hindus before converting to Sikhism, they disagreed about what should be done with the Guru's body. Hindus cremate their dead, while Muslims bury bodies facing in the direction of Mecca.

To decide what should be done, they agreed to place flowers on each side of the Guru's body. The group whose flowers lasted longest would get to choose what they did with Nanak's body. According to legend, when the followers returned the next morning, the Guru's body was missing, and both sets of flowers were as fresh as the moment they had been placed by his side. This story shows how Sikhs believe that Nanak was very special and that he spread his message of equality even in death.

> ### Fact
> During his time at Kartarpur, Nanak wrote 974 hymns, which were included in the Sikh scriptures after his death.

> ### Key vocabulary
> **bhai** A title given to people respected by Sikhs; it literally means 'brother'
>
> **caste** A series of social classes that determine someone's job and status in society
>
> **chapati** A type of flatbread commonly eaten in India and Pakistan
>
> **disciples** Followers of a religious leader
>
> **Kartarpur** A town in modern Pakistan where the first Sikh community was founded in 1522 by Guru Nanak

Check your understanding

1. How many great journeys did Guru Nanak make and where did he go?
2. What message did Nanak give to Muslims?
3. Describe the story of blood and milk in your own words. What might it show about Nanak?
4. Where was the first Sikh community established and what happened there?
5. Why was there a disagreement after Nanak died and what do the legends surrounding his death teach Sikhs?

Who are the Ten Gurus? Angad to Arjan

Who were the people who helped to establish, develop and defend Sikhism after Nanak's death?

Guru Angad (1539–52)

For 200 years after Nanak's death, the title of Guru was passed on to nine more men who became leaders of Sikhism. Each Guru advanced the tradition and added ideas to it.

Guru Nanak appointed his successor just before he died. Most people thought he would choose one of his sons, but instead Nanak selected his devoted follower Lehna. To make sure he was worthy of this honour, Nanak put Lehna through a series of tests. These included doing menial tasks like carrying bundles of grass and washing dirty clothes. Nanak's sons felt these tasks were beneath them, but Lehna did them without complaint. Nanak gave Lehna the name 'Angad', which translates to mean 'part of me', 'limb' or 'myself'. Angad's willingness to do the menial tasks teaches Sikhs that service and equality are important.

Angad was the second Sikh Guru, after Nanak.

> **Fact**
>
> Guru Angad is particularly remembered for developing a new script called Gurmukhi ('from the mouth of the Guru'), which became the written form of the Punjabi language. He also collected the 974 hymns of Guru Nanak together for the first time.

> **Fact**
>
> Many Sikhs consider the nine Gurus who came after Guru Nanak to be his spirit in nine different forms. Therefore, Nanak and subsequent Gurus are referred to in the **Guru Granth Sahib** as Nanak I, Nanak II, and so on.

Guru Am ar Das (1552–74)

Guru Amar Das was Sikh leader from 1552 until his death in 1574. He continued the work of Guru Angad by developing the **langar** (communal kitchen). He insisted that anyone who came to visit him must first go to the langar and eat. In one famous story, the Muslim Emperor Akbar came to visit Guru Amar Das. Some people felt that the emperor should be given special treatment, but Angad believed that all people should be treated equally, and said that Akbar must visit the langar before meeting with him. Akbar was very impressed by the langar and he established a good relationship with the Sikhs.

Guru Amar Das also forbade the Hindu practice of sati, where a woman would throw herself on her husband's funeral pyre. Guru Amar Das said that widows could remarry and encouraged female Sikhs to carry the message of the Gurus to others.

Sikhs still share langar today, five centuries after Guru Amar Das.

Guru Ram Das (1574–81)

The fourth Guru only led Sikhs for seven years, but during this time he laid the foundations for the city of Amritsar. This would later become the spiritual home of Sikhism (see page 122).

Guru Arjan (1581–1606)

Guru Arjan invited a Muslim, Hazrat Mian Mir, to lay the foundation stone of the Golden Temple.

Guru Arjan arranged for a great temple – the Harmandir Sahib, or Golden Temple – to be built at Amritsar. This remains the holiest place in the world for Sikhs. Guru Arjan also collected all the hymns and words of the first Gurus together for the first time. This collection became known as the **Adi Granth**, or 'first book'. Guru Arjan included some of his own new prayers and writings by Hindus and Muslims. In 1604, a copy was placed in the Harmandir Sahib.

Guru Arjan is also revered as the first Sikh **martyr**. In 1605, Emperor Akbar died. He had been a tolerant ruler and had been on friendly terms with the Sikhs. He was succeeded by his son, Jahangir, whose name means 'conqueror of the world'. In 1606, Jahangir's own son led a failed rebellion to try and overthrow him. Guru Arjan was accused of being involved in this rebellion. He and 200 others were executed by Jahangir.

Historians disagree over the exact details of Guru Arjan's death. Most Sikhs believe that it was a particularly cruel act in which Guru Arjan was forced to sit on a hot cooking plate while burning sand was poured over him. He was then boiled alive in water before being drowned in a river. This is an important event in Sikh history because the Gurus who came after Arjan realised their people could be persecuted, perhaps violently. The Gurus began to regard themselves as military as well as spiritual leaders. They felt their role was to protect Sikhs from persecution at the hands of the Mughals.

Key vocabulary

Adi Granth A collection of hymns and writings of the early Sikh Gurus, compiled by Guru Arjan; it means 'first book'

Guru Granth Sahib The Sikh holy book; the name means 'from the Guru's mouth'

langar A word meaning 'free kitchen', a communal eating area found in every Sikh place of worship

martyr Someone who is killed for his or her beliefs

Check your understanding

1 Who was Guru Nanak's successor and how was he chosen?

2 What happened when Emperor Akbar visited Guru Amar Das?

3 What else is Guru Amar Das remembered for doing?

4 Which holy site was built by Guru Arjan?

5 Describe the life and death of Guru Arjan. How might he provide inspiration for Sikhs today?

Unit 1: History and belief

Who are the Ten Gurus? Hargobind to Gobind Singh

The violent death of Guru Arjan left the future of Sikhism in the balance. How would the religion survive persecution?

Guru Hargobind (1606–44)

After the martyrdom of Guru Arjan, the title passed to Arjan's son, Hargobind. Guru Hargobind was only 11 years old when his father died, but he acted quickly, encouraging Sikhs to defend themselves. On being given the title Guru, he put on two swords. The first showed his spiritual authority (piri) as Guru and the second showed his worldly authority (miri) as a political and military leader. Miri piri requires a person to be a saint first and a soldier second. This means that a Sikh's saintliness and spirituality should come first, and this spirituality should guide the person in worldly matters. These ideas are reflected in the **Khanda**.

Guru Hargobind, the son of the fifth Guru, Arjan, the first Sikh martyr.

The Khanda

The symbol of Sikhism is called the Khanda, which contains three swords. Two curved swords cross over at the bottom. The right-hand sword reflects spiritual authority (piri) and the left-hand sword reflects worldly authority (miri). The sword in the middle is also called a khanda. It reminds Sikhs that it is their duty to fight for justice in the world. The circle in the middle is called a chakkar. It has two meanings. The spiritual meaning is that the circle represents God, who is eternal. The other meaning is a military one. Sikhs used sharp circular weapons called chakrams in battle.

Hargobind fought a series of battles against the Mughals, which ended with a great victory for the Sikhs at the Battle of Amritsar in 1634. Hargobind attracted many new followers to Sikhism and was the longest-serving Guru, leading Sikhs for almost 38 years.

Guru Har Rai (1644–61)

Guru Hargobind was succeeded by his grandson, Guru Har Rai. Although there were occasional conflicts with the Mughals during his time as Guru, this was generally a period of greater peace. The new Guru travelled around the Punjab spreading the message of equality first revealed to

Guru Nanak. Guru Har Rai is also believed to have provided medicines for the sick and established a hospital at Kiratpur. Just before he died, the Guru appointed his young son Har Krishan to succeed him.

Guru Har Krishan (1661–64)

Guru Har Krishan was only five years old when he became Guru and he died three years later, of smallpox. There was an epidemic of the disease at the time, and the Guru personally helped those suffering from it. Among Sikhs today, Guru Har Krishan is a popular example of childhood wisdom and innocence. Schools are sometimes named after him.

Guru Tegh Bahadur (1664–75)

The ninth Guru was the youngest son of Guru Hargobind. He went on a number of journeys throughout northern India, spreading the message of Sikhism. During Tegh Bahadur's time as Guru, the Mughals were led by the powerful Aurangzeb, who conquered new areas of central and southern India.

Guru Tegh Bahadur.

Aurangzeb decided he wanted Islam to be the only religion in his empire. He ordered that Hindus, Sikhs and people of other religions must convert to Islam and live under Shari'a (Islamic) law. He also ordered the destruction of thousands of Hindu temples and shrines. People who resisted these actions were killed or forced to become slaves.

Legend says that some Hindu religious teachers begged Guru Tegh Bahadur to help defend them. The Guru sent word to Emperor Aurangzeb that if he could convert the Guru to Islam, everyone else would convert, otherwise the Mughals should leave non-Muslims alone.

Aurangzeb summoned Guru Tegh Bahadur to Delhi. While travelling there, Guru Tegh Bahadur was captured by the Emperor's soldiers and brought to the city in chains. Records dating from about 100 years later say that Guru Tegh Bahadur was tortured for many weeks to try and get him to convert. When the Guru refused, he was forced to watch his companions be killed, and he was then publicly beheaded. Like Guru Arjan, Tegh Bahadur is revered by Sikhs today for sacrificing his life for his beliefs, and for fighting to protect the rights and beliefs of others.

The execution of Guru Tegh Bahadur and the expansion of the Mughal Empire under Aurangzeb was a dark time for Sikhs. However, the last of the Ten Gurus, Gobind Singh, was not going to let Sikhism be extinguished. He made it his business to defend his religion and avenge his father's brutal death.

Activity

Draw a grid of ten boxes. In each box, create a brief fact file for each of the ten Gurus.

Key vocabulary

Khanda The symbol of Sikhism, made up of two double-edged swords, one sword in the middle and a circle

Check your understanding

1 What is the meaning of the two swords worn by Guru Hargobind?
2 What is the Khanda?
3 What happened during the reign of the Emperor Aurangzeb?
4 Why was Guru Tegh Bahadur executed?
5 'It is right to die for your beliefs.' Discuss this statement, and refer to at least one Sikh martyr in your answer.

Unit 1: History and belief
Guru Gobind Singh and the Khalsa

How did Guru Gobind Singh change the future of Sikhism at the festival of Vaisakhi in 1699?

Guru Gobind Singh (1675–1708)

Tegh Bahadur's only son, Gobind Singh, was nine years old when his father was martyred. Being Guru was a daunting task, but he was guided by wise, older Sikhs. They helped him as he studied the holy texts of the Gurus and learned important military skills such as martial arts, horse riding, archery and battle strategy.

The origins of the Khalsa

In 1699, when Guru Gobind Singh was 30 years old, he arranged a dramatic event that changed Sikhism forever. At the annual spring festival of Vaisakhi, Gobind Singh called all Sikhs from across the region to gather together in Anandpur. Holding a khanda, he asked for a volunteer from the crowd who was willing to die for Sikhism. After a nervous pause, one man hesitantly came forward. The Guru took him into a tent and returned with his sword stained with blood. Blood could also be seen running along the ground. Gobind Singh called for more volunteers. One by one, four more men disappeared with the Guru. Each time the Guru returned, his sword was covered in fresh blood.

The people were shocked. They thought that the Guru had killed the five men to demonstrate the commitment required to be a Sikh. However, all the men were led out of the tent by the Guru alive and unharmed. Gobind Singh then **initiated** the five and called them the **Panj Pyare** ('the blessed/beloved ones'). In doing this, he was saying that those who were willing to die for the Sikh religion were holy and blessed by God. The Panj Pyare were the first members of a community known as the **Khalsa**, which means 'the brotherhood of the pure'.

After the Guru had initiated the Panj Pyare, he asked the five men to initiate him into the Khalsa too, as well as others in the crowd. They did this in what is now known as the Amrit ceremony.

Guru Gobind Singh.

Activity

Imagine you were at the founding of the Khalsa in 1699. Write an eyewitness report explaining what you saw and how people reacted to the events as they took place.

The Amrit ceremony

Many Sikhs today choose to join the Khalsa. Some do so when they are teenagers, but others wait until they are adults. To become part of the Khalsa, Sikhs must participate in the Amrit ceremony. Here, an iron bowl is filled with **amrit** (a mixture of sugar and water). This is then stirred with a khanda. Those Sikhs wishing to join the Khalsa drink some of the mixture and the remainder is sprinkled on their eyes and hair. They vow to show devotion to God and to the Gurus. Once they are members of the Khalsa, Sikhs wear five items known as the 'Five Ks' (see pages 104–105). The Amrit ceremony ends with a sweet food called **karah parshad** being shared among all the people present.

The Panj Pyare initiating Guru Gobind Singh into the Khalsa with amrit.

Sikh surnames

Men who join the Khalsa are given the surname Singh, which means 'lion'. Women who join are given the surname Kaur, meaning 'princess'. Originally, these names were meant to replace people's surnames, and today many initiated Sikhs will only use Kaur and Singh as their surname. Sikhs who are not initiated may use these titles as their surnames and pass them on to their children, even if the children have not formally joined the Khalsa. By taking the same surnames, Sikhs aim to show that everyone is equal.

The assassination of Guru Gobind Singh

One of the main duties of the first members of the Khalsa was to protect Sikhs from being persecuted by the Mughals. Between 1699 and 1708, all Guru Gobind Singh's sons were captured and executed or killed in battle. Emperor Aurangzeb died in 1707 and was succeeded by his son. In 1708, Guru Gobind Singh set out to try and make peace with the new emperor, but on the way he was assassinated.

As Guru Gobind Singh lay dying, he told his followers that he would be the last human Guru. He declared that the Sikh holy scriptures would become a living and eternal Guru for Sikhs after his death. The hymns of Guru Tegh Bahadur were added to the Adi Granth and it became known as the Guru Granth Sahib. Sikhs today revere it as the eleventh and final Guru.

Key vocabulary

amrit Sugar that is mixed into water using a sword; it is drunk at the Amrit ceremony where people become part of the Sikh Khalsa

initiated Made a member of a particular group through a special ceremony

karah parshad A sweet food shared at the end of the Amrit ceremony

Khalsa The community of Sikhs founded by the tenth Guru, Gobind Singh

Panj Pyare 'The blessed ones' – the first five men who volunteered to join the Khalsa

Check your understanding

1 Who was Guru Gobind Singh?

2 What happened at the festival of Vaisakhi in 1699?

3 What do the names Singh and Kaur mean?

4 What is the Amrit ceremony and why is it important to Sikhs?

5 'Guru Gobind Singh was the most important of the Sikh Gurus.' Discuss this statement.

What are the Five Ks?

Why do Khalsa Sikhs wear the Panj Kakaar (Five Ks)?

After the Khalsa was established in 1699, Guru Gobind Singh gave its members some rules to follow, which developed the teachings of previous Gurus. Many of these teachings focus on performing good deeds, including giving to those in need and earning an honest living. Guru Gobind Singh also said that drugs, smoking and alcohol, and piercings were strictly forbidden and that people's clothing should be simple and modest.

In addition to this, the Guru taught that Khalsa Sikhs must wear five key items that show their faith. These five things represent a Sikh's commitment to both spirituality and defending justice.

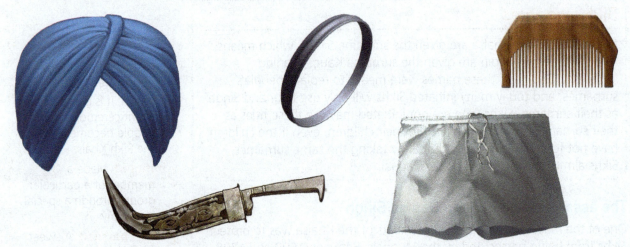

The five articles of faith are known as the Five Ks because their names in Punjabi all begin with the letter k.

Kesh (uncut hair)

Sikhs believe their bodies are a gift from God. As such, Khalsa Sikhs do not cut their hair. This is a sign of devotion to God and shows acceptance of what God has given them. In order to keep their hair tidy and clean, male members of the Khalsa wear a turban. At the time of the Gurus, turbans were worn by emperors and rulers. The Khalsa adopted the turban for two reasons. It showed that Khalsa Sikhs were powerful and it created a group identity for them, making members instantly recognisable.

Kangha (a wooden comb)

The kangha is a comb that has both a practical and spiritual purpose. The comb is used to keep the hair clean and tidy. Most members of the Khalsa will brush their hair twice a day. When it is not being worn, the kangha is tucked into the turban. The kangha also signifies the importance of discipline and reminds Sikhs that their lives, including work and family, should be well ordered.

Many devout members of the Khalsa believe the command not to cut hair relates to all bodily hair, and so do not cut or trim any hair on their face or body.

Kara (a simple steel bracelet)

The kara is a plain steel bracelet worn around the right wrist. It cannot be made of gold or silver, as these metals are too precious and not in keeping with the Gurus' teaching on equality. Steel is a strong metal, forged in fire, so the kara symbolises the strength required to be a Sikh and defend the religion. The kara also has spiritual significance. The circular shape represents the Sikh belief in monotheism by reflecting the eternity and oneness of God.

Kachera (special cotton underwear)

Kachera are loose-fitting shorts that both male and female members of the Khalsa wear under their clothes. Guru Gobind Singh is said to have told his followers to wear them because they made movement in battle easier. As such, kachera are a reminder to Sikhs that they should be ready to fight when others need help.

Fact

Sikhs prefer not to call the Five Ks 'symbols'. This is because the five items have a practical purpose as well as a religious meaning.

Kirpan (a short sword)

The kirpan is a sword worn by Khalsa Sikhs to remind them of their duty to defend their religion and fight for justice. The earliest members of the Khalsa would have carried full swords in order to fight against the Mughal Empire. Today, it is not practical to carry a full-size sword, so Sikhs often carry a small sword (held in a sheath).

The fifth of the Five Ks, the kirpan.

Activity

Draw and annotate an image of each of the Five Ks.

The kirpan and the law

In the UK, the law bans people from carrying knives, unless this is a religious requirement. It is estimated that fewer than 10 per cent of Sikhs in the UK wear a real kirpan. However, in times of heightened security because of terrorism, the issue of whether religious people should have the right to carry something that could be used as a weapon has caused much debate. Some security experts are concerned about the kirpan being carried in airports and other public places.

Check your understanding

1. How is a Khalsa Sikh different from other Sikhs?
2. Why do Sikh men wear turbans?
3. What are the Five Ks? Explain each in detail.
4. What problems might some Sikhs in the UK encounter when wearing the Five Ks?
5. 'All Sikhs should join the Khalsa.' Discuss this statement.

What is the Guru Granth Sahib?

Why do Sikhs treat the Guru Granth Sahib with such respect?

From Adi Granth to Guru Granth Sahib

The fifth Guru, Arjan, collected the Sikh scriptures into a volume known as the Adi Granth, which can be translated as 'first book' or 'first collection'. Arjan included the 974 hymns of Guru Nanak as well as other hymns written by Muslims and Hindus that were in keeping with Sikh beliefs. This book was greatly respected and it was placed inside the temple at Amritsar. When Gobind Singh was Guru, he added hymns that he and his father Guru Tegh Bahadur had written. As Gobind Singh died, he announced that this final collection, which had been put together over a period of nearly 150 years, would be given the title of 'Guru'.

The Guru Granth Sahib is the complete collection of Sikh scriptures.

Sikhs look to this holy book for guidance and leadership. Until 1864, all editions of the Guru Granth Sahib were carefully copied by hand. It was not until the twentieth century that printed editions were published.

Gurmukhi

When Guru Nanak began preaching the message that God had revealed to him, he used the spoken language of his homeland, Punjabi. However, when it came to writing down his message and hymns, Guru Angad created a new language, **Gurmukhi**, which means 'from the mouth of the Guru'. Some think this was because he wanted to establish Sikhism as a religion that was distinct from Hinduism and Islam, which also had many followers in India at this time.

Showing respect

Since the first printed editions, the Guru Granth Sahib has always had 1430 pages, which are known as 'angs' (limbs). All copies of the text are exactly the same and there are strict rules about how the book is printed. Any misprints or damaged copies must be formally cremated in the same way that the dead body of a Guru would be treated.

Most Sikhs would say that the only genuine versions of the Guru Granth Sahib are those that have been authorised, printed and published in Gurmukhi by people working in the holy complex in Amritsar. These versions are placed in Sikh **gurdwaras** and also in some homes. Sikhs do not worship the Guru Granth Sahib – it is not a god. However, they do show it the same respect they would show to a living Guru, and the book is given a room of its own in a house or gurdwara.

When is it used?

The Guru Granth Sahib is used during Sikh worship. It must also be present at important occasions such as weddings and the Amrit ceremony. At some Sikh festivals or important events, a **granthi** will read the whole text from start to finish. This is called an Akhand Path. The reading takes approximately 48 hours and is performed by a group of individuals who will each read for 2 hours. At the end of most Sikh worship services, the granthi will open the text at random and read a few verses to the congregation. These verses provide Sikhs with wisdom and guidance that they can take away and use in their everyday lives.

Transporting the Guru Granth Sahib

There are strict rules for distributing the authorised copies of the Guru Granth Sahib. For example, in 2004, when Canadian Sikhs required new copies of the Guru Granth Sahib, the books had to be flown from India. They were accompanied at all times by five members of the Khalsa, who carried the Gurus on their heads, while others prayed, chanted or fanned the sacred texts. On the plane, the books each had their own seat. As Sikhs have emigrated from the Punjab and settled in the West, there is an increasing demand for official copies of the Guru Granth Sahib. However, the only official printers remain in Amritsar.

Strict rules govern how copies of the holy book are transported from one place to another.

The Guru Granth Sahib in the digital age

The complete text of the Guru Granth Sahib is about 400,000 words. It is large and heavy, and so expensive to buy and difficult to store. Today, some Sikhs read the Guru Granth Sahib online. This can be particularly helpful for those learning Gurmukhi, as it means they can study at home as well as going to classes at the gurdwara.

Mool Mantar

Ik Onkaar Satnaam Kartaa Purakh Nirbhau Nirvair
Akaal Moorat Ajooni Saibhang Gurprasaad.

Key vocabulary

granthi People who read from, and look after, the Guru Granth Sahib; Sikhs do not have priests or religious leaders and anyone can read from the Guru Granth Sahib

gurdwara The Sikh place of worship; it literally means 'doorway to the Guru'

Gurmukhi A language created by the Gurus and used to write the Guru Granth Sahib

Check your understanding

1 What is the Guru Granth Sahib?
2 Why is the Guru Granth Sahib written in Gurmukhi?
3 How and why do Sikhs treat the Guru Granth Sahib as a person?
4 Who is able to print authorised copies? Why do you think this is?
5 Why might some Sikhs say reading the Guru Granth Sahib online is not the same as reading a printed version?

Unit 1: History and belief

What do Sikhs believe about God?

How do Sikhs describe God and what do they base their ideas on?

The Mool Mantra

The key text for understanding Sikh beliefs about God is the **Mool Mantra**, which Sikhs consider to be a complete summary of all teaching about God. It is repeated more than 100 times in the Guru Granth Sahib. Sikhs often use it as a prayer.

Ik Onkar are the first words of the Mool Mantra and a popular Sikh symbol.

Words (in Gurmukhi)	Translation
Ik Onkar	There is only one God
Sat Nam	Eternal truth is his name
Karta Purakh	He is the creator
Nir Bhau	He is without fear
Nir Vair	He is without hate
Akal Murat	Immortal, without form
Ajuni	Beyond birth and death
Saibhang	He is the enlightener
Gur Prasaad	He can be reached through the mercy and grace of the true Guru

> ### Fact
>
> The first words of the Mool Mantra, 'Ik Onkar', are often displayed inside gurdwaras or people's homes. This is to remind Sikhs that there is one God and his message can be found in the Guru Granth Sahib.

In the Mool Mantra, God is described as immortal, the creator, without form, and being beyond life and death. God is the cause of creation and does not appear in human form. Most Sikhs believe that we can describe God through language, but ultimately he is so great that he is beyond human comprehension. Humans cannot define him in words. Sikhs believe that the best way to understand what God is like is through the lives and example of the Gurus and the teachings found in the Guru Granth Sahib. They also believe they can come to know God and develop a personal relationship with him through prayer and service to others.

The Ik Onkar can sometimes be found on Sikhs' mobile phone covers.

God's name

In the Guru Granth Sahib, there are different names given to the same God. Sikhs believe that it is particularly respectful to repeat the name of God over and over again in prayer. This is called **naam japna**.

> The naam japna form of worship comes from Guru Nanak's words in the Guru Granth Sahib:
>
> 66 If I had 100,000 tongues, and these were then multiplied twenty times more, with each tongue, I would repeat, hundreds of thousands of times, the Name of the One, the Lord of the Universe. 99
>
> Guru Granth Sahib 7:6–7

The most commonly used name for God in Sikhism is **Waheguru**, which translates as 'wonderful Lord' or 'wonderful Guru'. The term appears in the Guru Granth Sahib 16 times, but is used by Sikhs in prayer and meditation as a way of expressing God's ultimate power and reality.

The name of Waheguru also plays a central role in the Amrit ceremony. When a person is initiated as a Khalsa Sikh, he or she will take the amrit (blessed water) and repeat the following five times: 'Waheguru ji ka Khalsa, Waheguru ji ki Fateh.' This means 'Hail the Khalsa who belongs to the Lord God! Hail the Lord God to whom belongs the victory!' Some Sikhs will also use this phrase as a personal greeting when they meet other Sikhs for the first time or when they meet someone they consider to be particularly holy.

> 66 You have formed and created this play, this great game. O Waheguru, this is all your own making. The Lord is Inaccessible, Infinite, Eternal and Primordial; no one knows His beginning. 99
>
> Guru Granth Sahib 1404:2

The language used by the Gurus to describe God is poetic and its meaning is not always clear. God is described in the Guru Granth Sahib as personal, someone as close to you as your family, but at the same time omnipotent (all powerful) and omnipresent (everywhere). This highlights that for many Sikhs God remains a mystery to be pondered:

Sikhs at worship.

> 66 You are my Father, and You are my Mother. You are my Relative, and You are my Brother. You are my Protector everywhere; why should I feel any fear or anxiety? 99
>
> Guru Granth Sahib 103:12–13

Key vocabulary

Mool Mantra The first hymn written by Guru Nanak; it summarises Sikh beliefs about God

naam japna Repeating the name of God over and over as an act of worship

Waheguru the most common name used by Sikhs to describe God meaning 'wonderful Lord/Guru'

Check your understanding

1 What is the Mool Mantra and what does it teach Sikhs about God?
2 Where might you find the Ik Onkar?
3 How do Sikhs believe they can know God?
4 What is meant by Waheguru and when might Sikhs use this name?
5 What might be the advantages and difficulties of seeing God as a mystery?

Knowledge organiser

Key vocabulary

Adi Granth A collection of hymns and writings of the early Sikh Gurus, compiled by Guru Arjan; it means 'first book'

amrit Sugar that is mixed into water using a sword; it is drunk at the Amrit ceremony

Amrit ceremony Ceremony to become part of the Sikh Khalsa

Bhai A title given to people respected by Sikhs; it literally means 'brother'

caste A series of social classes that determine someone's job and status in society

chapati A type of flatbread commonly eaten in India and Pakistan

disciples Followers of a religious leader

The Five Ks Five articles of faith worn by the Khalsa: kesh (uncut hair), kangha (a wooden comb), kara (a steel bracelet), kachera (special cotton underwear) and kirpan (a short sword)

granthi People who read from, and look after, the Guru Granth Sahib; Sikhs do not have religious leaders or priests and anyone can read from the Guru Granth Sahib

gurdwara The Sikh place of worship; it literally means 'doorway to the Guru'

Gurmukhi A language created by the Gurus and used to write the Guru Granth Sahib

Guru A religious teacher or guide who leads a follower from spiritual ignorance (*Gu*, 'darkness') into spiritual enlightenment (*ru*, 'light')

Guru Granth Sahib The Sikh holy book; the name means 'from the Guru's mouth'

initiated Made a member of a particular group through a special ceremony

Janam Sakhis Stories about the childhood and life of Guru Nanak

karah parshad A sweet food shared at the end of the Amrit ceremony

Kartarpur A town in modern Pakistan where the first Sikh community was founded in 1522 by Guru Nanak

Kaur 'Princess' – the title given to a female Khalsa Sikh

Khalsa The community of Sikhs founded by the tenth Guru, Gobind Singh

khanda The symbol of Sikhism, made up of two double-edged swords, one sword in the middle and a circle

langar A word meaning 'free kitchen'; a communal eating area found in every Sikh place of worship

martyr Someone who is killed for his or her beliefs

monotheist Someone who believes in only one God

Mool Mantra The first hymn written by Guru Nanak; it summarises Sikh beliefs about God

Mughal Empire The rulers of the area that is now India and Pakistan in the sixteenth and seventeenth centuries

naam japna Repeating the name of God over and over as an act of worship

Panj Pyare 'The blessed ones' – the first five men who volunteered to join the Khalsa

revelation A message revealed by God to humans

Sikh A follower of Sikhism; it comes from the Sanskrit word *shishya*, which means 'disciple' or 'learner'

Singh 'Lion' – the title given to a male Khalsa Sikh

Waheguru the most common name used by Sikhs to describe God meaning 'wonderful Lord/Guru'

Key facts

- There are around 25 million Sikhs in the world today, most of them (19 million) living in India.

- Sikhism began with a man called Nanak, who was born in part of India called the Punjab.

- When Nanak was 30 he received a revelation in which he understood that although there are many different religions there is only one God. God loves all people equally, whatever religion they follow.

- Stories about Nanak's childhood and life are collected in the Janam Sakhis.

- Nanak made four long journeys over a period of 20 years, spreading word of his revelation. He visited and talked with Buddhists, Hindus and Muslims.

- The story of the miracle of milk and blood emphasises one of Guru Nanak's important teachings – that of working hard and honestly.

- Guru Nanak died in 1539. He was followed by nine Sikh Gurus, who developed the Sikh tradition.

- Guru Arjan is famous for building the holiest site in the world for Sikhs, the Harmandir Sahib, and for being the first Sikh martyr after his death at the hands of the Mughals.

- The Sikh symbol of the Khanda was established by Guru Hargobind, who put on two swords to indicate his spiritual authority (piri) and his worldly authority (miri).

- The ninth Guru was Tegh Bahadur, who challenged the Mughal Emperor Aurangzeb to convert him to Islam. When the emperor failed to do so, he had the Guru executed.

- The last of the human Gurus was Gobind Singh, who established the Khalsa, a brotherhood of Sikhs established to protect their people from persecution.

- Male Sikhs who join the Khalsa take the surname Singh ('lion') and female Khalsa Sikhs take the surname Kaur ('princess').

- Before he died, Gobind Singh said that the collection of Sikh holy scriptures, the Guru Granth Sahib, would be the eleventh and final – eternal – Guru.

- The Guru Granth Sahib is a collection of scriptures collected over 150 years that is highly revered by Sikhs, who look to it for guidance and leadership.

- It is written in a language called Gurmukhi and there are strict rules about how copies of it can be printed, transported and treated.

- The book is used during Sikh worship services and during special ceremonies. Sometimes readers called granthi will read the whole text from start to finish, which takes about 48 hours.

- The Mool Mantra is a text that describes Sikh beliefs about God, including that he is the creator, immortal, without fear or hate, and beyond birth and death.

Key people

Akbar A Muslim Mughal emperor and ruler who was very impressed by the langar and had a good relationship with the Sikhs

Aurangzeb A Mughal emperor during Tegh Bahadur's time as Guru; he had Guru Tegh Bahadur killed

Guru Nanak (1469–1539) The founder and first Guru of Sikhism

Guru Angad (1539–52) A devoted follower of Nanak who succeeded him as second Guru

Guru Amar Das (1552–74) The third Guru

Guru Ram Das (1574–81) The fourth Guru

Guru Arjan (1581–1606) The fifth Guru, who created the Adi Granth (first Sikh scriptures) and founded the Golden Temple in Amritsar; he was martyred by the Mughal emperor

Guru Hargobind (1606–44) The sixth Guru; a key military leader

Guru Har Rai (1644–61) The seventh Guru

Guru Har Krishan (1661–64) The eighth Guru, who died at the age of eight

Guru Tegh Bahadur (1664–1675) The ninth Guru; executed by the Mughal emperor

Guru Gobind Singh (1675–1708) The tenth and final human Guru, who established the Khalsa

Jahangir A son of Mughal Emperor Akbar who had Guru Arjan killed

Lalo A hard-working carpenter of low caste who became one of the first Sikhs

Malik Bhago A rich and corrupt man who was angered by Guru Nanak eating with Lalo

Sikhism in the modern world

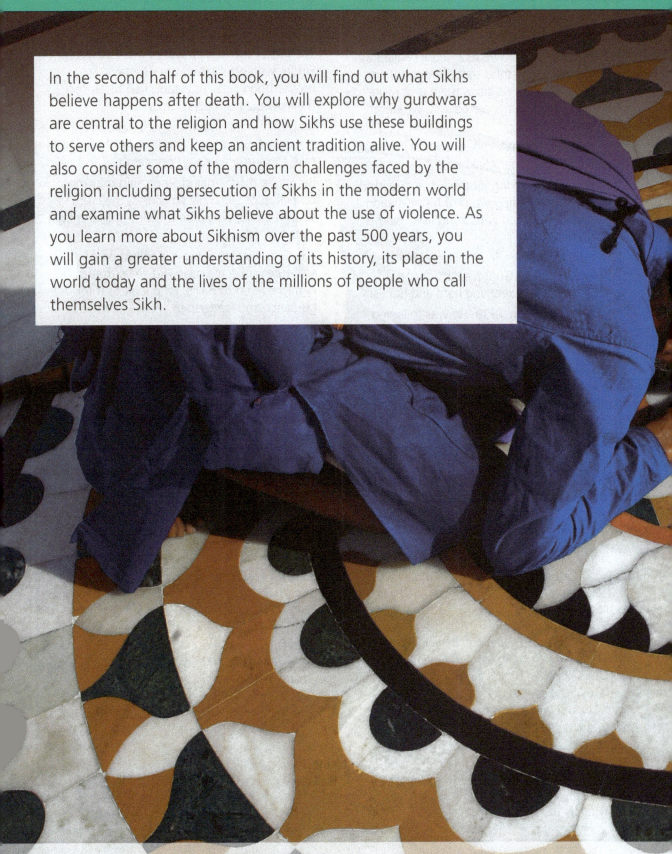

In the second half of this book, you will find out what Sikhs believe happens after death. You will explore why gurdwaras are central to the religion and how Sikhs use these buildings to serve others and keep an ancient tradition alive. You will also consider some of the modern challenges faced by the religion including persecution of Sikhs in the modern world and examine what Sikhs believe about the use of violence. As you learn more about Sikhism over the past 500 years, you will gain a greater understanding of its history, its place in the world today and the lives of the millions of people who call themselves Sikh.

What do Sikhs believe happens after death?

What do Sikhs believe happens after we die and how is this reflected in Sikh funerals?

The law of karma

Like Hindus and Buddhists, Sikhs believe that everyone is in a cycle of birth, death and rebirth. A person's rebirth is decided by God based on the law of **karma**. People can create good karma by worshipping God and performing good deeds. Those who live selfishly and ignore the message of the Gurus will produce bad karma and achieve a lower rebirth, even returning as an animal. For Sikhs, the goal of life is to escape the cycle of birth, death and rebirth by achieving **mukti**. This is the union of the soul (**atma**) with God.

Sikhs believe that everything that seems real to us is in fact an illusion (**maya**). This does not mean that our experiences of family, friends, relationships, emotions, money and possessions are false, but that that they will not last. Sikhs believe that although things in this world appear real, the only thing that is eternal and therefore ultimately true is Waheguru.

Sikhs believe that we should try to escape maya and achieve mukti. The Guru Granth Sahib explains how this can be done (see margin).

The first sentence of these verses shows that it is God who decides whether someone will be reborn or whether he or she will find mukti. Most Sikh scholars agree that mukti can be achieved by combining human effort with the grace of God ('Those who receive his Mercy obtain the True One').

The word Gurmukh refers to someone who puts God and the teaching of the Gurus at the centre of his or her life. A Gurmukh will hope to achieve mukti through 'true actions'. These include naam japna (reciting God's name), kirat karna – earning an honest living) and vand chakna (selfless service involving giving to those in need). These are actions that produce good karma.

When Sikhs become attached to worldly possessions, they are said to be a **Manmukh** (someone who is self-centred). They may show signs of the five vices:

- ahankar (pride)
- kam (lust or desire)
- krodh (anger)
- lobh (greed)
- moh (attachment)

These vices encourage unethical behaviour. They can stop people from achieving release from the cycle of birth, death and rebirth.

Peoples' rebirths depend on their karma.

Rebirth — **Cycle of Life** — Birth

Death

The goal of life is to escape this cycle and for the soul to join God.

> 66 Those who are protected by the Guru are saved; all others are cheated and plundered by deceitful worldly affairs. Love dies, and affection vanishes. Hatred and alienation die. Entanglements end, and egotism dies, along with attachment to Maya, possessiveness and anger. Those who receive His Mercy obtain the True One. The **Gurmukhs** dwell forever in balanced restraint. By true actions, the True Lord is met, and the Guru's Teachings are found. Then, they are not subject to birth and death; they do not come and go in reincarnation. 99
> Guru Granth Sahib 19:10–12

Funerals

A Sikh funeral is called an Antam Sanskar. Sikhs believe that, because death is not the end, people should not grieve too much when a loved one dies. The Guru Granth Sahib says that everything that lives must die, and Sikhs find comfort in the noble way that Guru Nanak and other Gurus (particularly the martyrs) faced death.

A Sikh funeral.

Traditionally, Sikh funerals took place on the same day that someone died, or as soon as possible afterwards. Today, however, funerals might take place between three and seven days after death.

Before the funeral, the body is washed and dressed in clean clothes. The hair is covered by a turban or a traditional scarf and the body is then cremated. If the person wore the Five Ks in life, then these are cremated. In India, the body would be cremated on an open funeral pyre. However, this is illegal in the UK, so Sikh funerals take place at a crematorium. At every Sikh funeral, mourners recite the **Kirtan Sohila**. This is a prayer said by Sikhs every evening before they sleep. It reminds them that death comes to all and that Sikhs long to be united with God.

After a cremation in India, the family usually scatters the ashes in open water. In the UK, Sikhs may scatter ashes into flowing rivers, but they must get permission from their local council to do so. Sikhs do not built monuments over the remains of their dead. Mourning can last for 10 days, during which an entire reading of the Guru Granth Sahib may take place. The mourning is ended by the sharing of karah parshad (see page 103).

❝ My friends, give me your blessings that I may merge with my Lord and Master. Unto each and every home, into each and every heart, this summons is sent out; the call comes each and every day. ❞

Kirtan Sohila

Key vocabulary

atma The soul

Gurmukh Someone who put God and the teachings of the Gurus at the centre of life

karma The forces that influence people's future rebirth

Kirtan Sohila An evening prayer that is also said during a Sikh funeral

Manmukh Someone who is self-centred and does not put God at the centre of life

Maya The temporary and illusory nature of the world

mukti Union with Waheguru; to escape the world of illusion and the cycle of life, death and rebirth

Check your understanding

1. What do Sikhs believe happens when people die? Include and explain a quotation from the Guru Granth Sahib in your answer.
2. What do Sikhs mean when they say that the world in which we live is maya?
3. What are the five vices?
4. Explain what happens at a Sikh funeral.
5. Why might death be seen as a time of hope for Sikhs? Include a quotation from the Kirtan Sohila in your answer.

What is a gurdwara?

How are Sikh beliefs expressed in a gurdwara?

The Sikh place of worship is called a gurdwara, which means 'doorway to the Guru'. The gurdwara is where the Guru Granth Sahib lives, and so Sikhs go there to hear the teachings of the Gurus.

Gurdwaras are open for anyone to visit, whether they are Sikhs or not. However, there are rules about how people must behave inside the gurdwara. All visitors must act respectfully, including removing their shoes and covering their head before entering the main hall. Visitors are not allowed to bring alcohol, tobacco or drugs into any part of the building.

The first gurdwara was built in Kartarpur by Guru Nanak in 1521. Some gurdwaras are built especially for Sikh worship (such as the Haramdir Sahib, or Golden Temple, in Amritsar), whereas others, particularly outside India, are in converted buildings or houses. However big or small a gurdwara, they all share certain features.

The Nishan Sahib

One way of spotting a gurdwara is by the flag – called the **Nishan Sahib** – that flies above it. This is usually orange with a picture of a khanda. During the early days of Sikhism, the flag would have been particularly important, as it would have shown passers-by that the building was a safe place for Sikhs and other people.

The Diwan Hall

The main room in the gurdwara is called the **Diwan Hall**. This is where services and ceremonies take place, such as weddings and initiations into the Khalsa.

The main focus of the hall is a throne at the front – the **takht**. The takht is modelled on the throne of an Indian king at the time of the Gurus and it is often covered with a special cloth. However, the throne is not for a human to sit on – it is for the Guru Granth Sahib. The holy book is treated with the same devotion and respect as a human Guru. When it is not in use it is kept in its own room. Each day it is carried above people's heads from this room to the Diwan Hall in a sacred procession. During a service, a granthi waves a special fan called a **chauri** over the Guru Granth Sahib. This practice dates back to the time of the Indian royal court, where kings and other rulers would be kept cool by someone fanning them. As such, the chauri is a symbol of respect and authority.

It might seem that during their services Sikhs are worshipping a book, but this is not the case. Sikhs believe that God alone is worthy of worship.

> 66 Through the Gurdwara, the Guru's Gate, one obtains understanding. By being washed through this Gate, it becomes pure. 99
> Guru Granth Sahib 730:1–2

The flag outside a gurdwara flies at the top of a pole, which is usually wrapped in orange fabric.

The Guru Granth Sahib is carried above the head as a sign of respect.

For this reason, many gurdwaras will contain no statues or bells, as these are seen as a distraction from worship. Often the only images in a gurdwara are paintings of the Gurus or famous gurdwaras.

Equality in the gurdwara

The Sikh belief in equality is evident throughout the gurdwara. There are no religious leaders or priests in the Sikh tradition. The granthi can be a man or a woman, as long as he or she is fluent in Gurmukhi and trained in looking after the Guru Granth Sahib. When people enter the Diwan Hall, they bow to Guru Granth Sahib, and then sit down on the floor. Only the ill or the elderly use chairs. Sitting on the floor shows that everyone is equal. It also shows respect and humility, because it means that worshippers are lower than the Guru Granth Sahib. Traditionally, men and women sit separately on either side of the hall, but this is not a requirement. At the end of every service, or perhaps during the service, karah parshad is shared among everybody equally.

In the Gurdwara worshippers sit on the floor as a sign of equality.

Activity

Using the description above to help you, draw a design for a Gurdwara.

Key vocabulary

chauri A fan traditionally used by rulers but now waved over the Guru Granth Sahib as a sign of respect

Diwan Hall The main hall in a gurdwara, where worship services take place

Nishan Sahib A flag that flies over every gurdwara

takht The throne on which the Guru Granth Sahib is placed each day for services in the gurdwara

Check your understanding

1. What does the word gurdwara mean?
2. What can be seen outside every gurdwara?
3. What would you do when entering a gurdwara?
4. Explain how the Guru Granth Sahib is shown respect in the gurdwara.
5. How is equality demonstrated in the gurdwara?

Unit 2: Sikhism in the modern world
What is the langar?

How does the langar ensure that the Gurdwara is a place of charity and service as well as worship?

Unlike most other places of worship, gurdwaras must contain somewhere for people to cook and share food. This part of the gurdwara is called the langar. The food made and served here is also called langar.

The langar is open to everyone, regardless of gender, ethnicity, caste or religion. For this reason, all the food that is prepared and served in it is vegetarian. Everyone receives the same food. It is often vegetarian dahl (lentil curry) served with yoghurt and rice or chapatti bread. Sikhs are expected to volunteer at the langar by donating, cooking and serving food, as well as washing up and cleaning. This is a key part of what Sikhs refer to as **sewa**.

> 66 Sikh identity is tied up with food and service to such an extent that the main motto in the eighteenth and nineteenth centuries was 'victory to the cooking pot and the sword, to charity and to justice.' 99
>
> Jasvir Singh, a British Sikh who is a lawyer and co-chair of the Faiths Forum for London

A langar in a gurdwara.

Sikh beliefs in equality are also shown by the seating arrangements in the langar. Traditionally, people sat on the floor to eat so that everyone was at the same level, with no one in a higher position. Today, this is still the case in some gurdwaras, but in others people sit on benches. In the langar, people sit in rows rather than around a table. Again, this is to show that no one is more important than anyone else. Men and women eat side by side in the langar.

The langar for the community

Some experts claim that in recent years many non-Sikhs have started to rely on the langar for food. In 2013, The Sikh Federation UK estimated that approximately 5,000 meals were being served to non-Sikhs in Britain's gurdwaras each week. Homeless people and others who live in poverty often go to a gurdwara for a daily meal, and most Sikhs welcome them.

However, not everyone in need lives close enough to a gurdwara to visit the langar, or knows about it. Some Sikhs, such as the Sikh Welfare and Awareness Team (SWAT), have taken the idea of the free kitchen to the streets. SWAT makes three trips a week to feed the homeless in central London. It is estimated that they help at least 250 homeless people each

Fact

The langar in the Golden Temple is the largest free kitchen in the world and regularly feeds up to 100,000 people on a daily basis. This number can double or triple during Sikh festivals.

week by serving langar and handing out water, chocolate bars and other supplies such as toiletries and sleeping bags. They do this to follow three pillars of Guru Nanak's teaching:

- naam japna (remembering God, reciting God's name)
- kirat karna (earning an honest living)
- vand chakana (selflessly serving others, sharing income and resources)

Activity

Write a magazine article about the work of SWAT.

Young members of SWAT, a charity that helps the homeless.

International Langar Week

In October each year, Sikhs in the UK and around the world mark International Langar Week. During this time, Sikhs are asked to try and do three things:

- introduce a friend to the langar
- set up a langar in a public place
- join a local street langar team that gives food to the poor.

A traditional langar meal.

In 2016, the hashtag for this week was #HelloLangarGoodbyeWorldHunger.

Key vocabulary

sewa Selfless service to others

Check your understanding

1. What are the two meanings of langar?
2. How did the langar begin? Refer to the Gurus in your answer.
3. What happens in the langar?
4. What three teachings of Guru Nanak are followed by the charity SWAT?
5. Explain how some Sikhs in the UK have taken langar to the wider community.

Unit 2: Sikhism in the modern world

How do Sikhs serve others?

Service to others starts in the langar, but how do Sikhs fulfil their mission to work for the benefit of others whenever and wherever they can?

Serving others (sewa) is a key Sikh belief. An obvious way in which Sikhs can perform sewa is through the langar found in every gurdwara. However, Sikhs can perform sewa in a number of other ways. These can be put into three categories.

> 66 One who performs selfless service, without thought of reward, shall attain his Lord and Master. 99
>
> Guru Granth Sahib 286:19

1. Tan (physical service)

> 66 Serving them, my body is purified. I wave the fans over them, and carry water for them; I grind the corn for them, and washing their feet, I am overjoyed. 99
>
> Guru Granth Sahib 518:14–15

One way in which Sikhs can perform sewa is through practical work. This might involve having a job that helps others, for example, being a doctor or a teacher. Many Sikhs are inspired to do **tan** by a legendary story about Guru Gobind Singh and the Khalsa fighting against the Mughal Empire. During the battle, a Sikh soldier was spotted giving water to a wounded enemy. Guru Gobind Singh called the man forward. The soldier tried to defend himself by telling the Guru that he saw no difference between friends and foes: 'Their faces were all the same for me.' The Sikh soldiers expected the Guru to tell him off, but instead he praised the man, exclaiming: 'Well done. You acted like a true Sikh.' The Guru then gave ointment to the soldier so that he could tend the wounds of all the wounded, both Sikh and non-Sikh.

Indian devotees wash utensils as sewa at the Golden temple in Amritsar.

2. Man (mental service)

> 66 As you serve Him [God], you will become like Him, as you walk according to His Will. 99
>
> Guru Granth Sahib 549:11

The name given to sewa that is performed through thought and words rather than direct action is **man**. An example might be reading the Guru Granth Sahib and talking about it to others, both Sikh and non-Sikh. Some Sikh families will read stories of the Sikh Gurus to their children, and this is considered mental service. Sikh students in schools might share knowledge of their faith in RE lessons or assemblies. Sikhs are not concerned with converting people to their religion. They believe the best way of showing their faith is by talking to others and sharing the beliefs that religions have in common.

3. Dhan (material service)

The third form of sewa is **dhan**. This is giving charity to those in need and can be done by offering money, making donations or volunteering time. Sikhs remember the tests Guru Nanak used when choosing his successor (see page 98) and believe that that no one is above doing menial work to help others.

Sikh students in a lesson at school.

> 66 He does not give anything in charity or generosity, and he does not serve the Saints; his wealth does not do him any good at all. 99
>
> Guru Granth Sahib 172:14

Khalsa Aid

Khalsa Aid is a charity that puts Sikh beliefs about sewa into practice. It was founded in 1999 by a British Sikh called Ravinder Singh and its motto is taken from a saying of Guru Gobind Singh: 'Recognise the whole human race as one.' The charity works to provide both short-term and long-term aid to people in need. It acts in response to tragedies such as the global refugee crisis and sends aid to people affected by natural disasters. In 2014, Ravinder Singh won the Sikh of the Year award at a ceremony in Amritsar.

Khalsa Aid's long-term projects include helping the poor in the Punjab with food relief and running a school in Amritsar. It also works in the UK. For example, during the winter floods of 2015 and early 2016, Khalsa Aid served food to people who had been forced to flee their homes and to the emergency services who were helping them. In a television interview, Ravinder Singh said: 'I am a man of action. I don't do meetings; I don't sit around tables: I see what needs doing and I do it.'

Sikhs providing aid during a disaster.

Key vocabulary

dhan Material sewa

man Mental sewa

tan Physical sewa

Check your understanding

1 What is sewa?

2 What are the three different forms of sewa?

3 What does the Guru Granth Sahib say about the importance of sewa?

4 Describe the work of Khalsa Aid.

5 'Sewa is the most important part of being a Sikh.' Discuss this statement.

The Golden Temple of Amritsar

Why is Amritsar a place of religious and historical significance for Sikhs?

The Golden Temple is one of the most famous buildings in the world. It is visited by approximately 5.5 million people every year. Many are Sikhs, but others are non-Sikhs and tourists. The temple is known to tourists as the Golden Temple, but Sikhs usually call it the Harmandir Sahib ('God's Temple'). It is the holiest site in the world for Sikhs and a popular **pilgrimage** destination.

The Golden Temple at Amritsar.

> ### Fact
>
> The temple has four entrances. These symbolise the Sikh belief that God sees everything and is everywhere in the world. They are also to show that the temple welcomes everyone, regardless of their caste, religion or where they come from.

Who built the Golden Temple?

In 1577, the fourth Guru, Ram Das, expanded an already existing pool of water so that Sikhs had somewhere to bathe. This pool still surrounds the temple today and is called the **sarovar**. Sikhs believe the water around the temple is holy and refer to it as immortal nectar. They think that bathing in these waters will cleanse them both physically and spiritually. Some Sikhs even claim that the waters have miraculous power that can cure people of illness.

The temple was designed and completed by the fifth Guru, Arjan, and the foundation stone was laid by a Muslim to demonstrate Sikh belief in religious freedom and equality. In 1604, Guru Arjan placed a copy of the Adi Granth inside the Harmandir Sahib. When later teachings were added to make this book the Guru Granth Sahib, this replaced the Adi Granth in the temple. Today, the temple is home to three copies of the Guru Granth Sahib.

> ### Fact
>
> The Harmandir Sabib was originally built of stone. It was not covered with gold until the early 1800s, when a Sikh ruler named Maharaja Ranjit Singh used his wealth and power to add gold to the inside and outside of the building.

A Sikh bathes in the holy sarovar that surrounds the Golden Temple.

> ### Activity
>
> Create an advert or travel brochure for the Golden Temple. Highlight the beautiful architecture and historical importance of the site.

The Amritsar Massacre

Amritsar was intended to be a place of worship, peace and religious equality. However, in the twentieth century, it became a site of violence and tragedy. In 1919, India was part of the British Empire, but an increasing number of Indian people were calling for independence and self-rule. On 13 April 1919, on the outskirts of the temple complex, British troops fired on a crowd of unarmed Indian protesters, killing 379 of them and wounding over 1000 more. The incident is known as the Amritsar Massacre. Many people believe that this event was one reason for the rise of a new movement, led by Mahatma Gandhi, that campaigned for independence in non-violent ways. In 2013, the British Prime Minister David Cameron visited Amritsar and referred to the massacre as 'a deeply shameful event in British history'.

Operation Blue Star

For centuries, some people believed that the Punjab should be a homeland for Sikhs and be ruled by them. However, when Britain granted India independence in 1947, it split the Punjab and created two separate countries: Pakistan and India. Pakistan was created as a home for Muslims and India for Hindus. Many Sikhs felt their national and religious identity had been ignored. Sikh nationalist movements grew over the following years, leading to violence at the Harmandir Sahib on 1–8 June 1984 in a military operation known as Operation Blue Star.

This memorial in Amritsar remembers the victims of the massacre.

A Sikh leader called Jarnail Singh Bhindranwale and hundreds of his followers armed themselves with weapons and occupied areas around the temple complex, demanding rights for Sikhs. The Indian Prime Minister Indira Gandhi ordered the army to clear the protestors from the temple. This resulted in the deaths of thousands of civilians as well as government troops. There was also severe damage to many of the temple's buildings, which had to be either repaired or completely rebuilt.

On 31 October 1984, Indira Gandhi was assassinated by two of her Sikh bodyguards. This led to a wave of anti-Sikh riots across India and many thousands of Sikhs were killed. Many Sikhs today still feel resentment at the way they were treated during these events. Some are still seeking justice. However, in recent years, things have begun to change. In 2004, a Sikh, Manmohan Singh, became the first non-Hindu Indian Prime Minister. He led the country until 2014.

Key vocabulary

pilgrimage A journey taken to a place of religious importance

sarovar The pool of water that surrounds the Golden Temple

Check your understanding

1. What is the Harmandir Sahib?
2. What is the symbolic meaning of the Golden Temple's design?
3. Why is the Harmandir called the Golden Temple?
4. Describe the events of the Amritsar Massacre in 1919.
5. What was Operation Blue Star and what happened in India as a result of it?

Unit 2: Sikhism in the modern world
Sikh festivals

What happens at Sikh festivals, and why?

Every year, Sikhs celebrate several important festivals, including the births and deaths of the Ten Gurus, **Vaisakhi** and Bandi Chhor Diwas, which falls on the same day as the Hindu festival Diwali.

Vaisakhi

Vaisakhi marks the beginning of the Sikh new year and is one of the most important days for Sikhs. It is celebrated on 13 or 14 April. Vaisakhi was a Hindu festival marking the spring harvest in the Punjab. However, it has added significance for Sikhs because it was during this festival in 1699 that Guru Gobind Singh founded the Khalsa (see page 103). On this day in India there are major celebrations at Anandpur, where the first five members of the Khalsa were initiated, and at the Harmandir Sahib in Amritsar, the spiritual home of Sikhism. Many Sikhs also choose to be initiated and take part in the Amrit ceremony during Vaisakhi.

Sikhs celebrating Vaisakhi.

Sikhs around the world celebrate the festival by visiting the gurdwara. The Nishan Sahib (the sacred orange flag found outside every Sikh temple) is taken down and replaced and the flagpole is washed in milk, yogurt and water. There are often also parades, community events, and even a procession of the Guru Granth Sahib around the local area led by five volunteers dressed up as Panj Pyare ('the blessed ones').

Bandi Chhor Diwas

The festival of Diwali is celebrated by followers of Hinduism for many different reasons. The date is not fixed, as Hindu festivals are based on the lunar calendar, but it usually takes place between mid-October and early November. Sikhs also celebrate on this day, but many of them call this festival Bandi Chhor Diwas.

For Sikhs, this festival is associated with the sixth Guru, Guru Hargobind, who was a strong military leader at a time of great danger to the early Sikhs. It is said that Guru Hargobind had been imprisoned by the Mughal emperor for failing to pay a fine given to his father, Guru Arjan. At Diwali, the emperor decided to release the Guru as a gesture of goodwill and to gain favour with the people he had conquered. Hargobind refused to leave unless the 52 Hindu kings who were being held as prisoners in his cell were also released. As a way of mocking this request, the emperor said that he would free as many kings as could hold on to the Guru's clothes. Guru Hargobind asked his guards to bring him a long cloak with many tassels. All 52 princes managed to hold on to the cloak and leave. This is where the name Bandi Chhor Diwas comes from – it means 'prisoner release day'.

Sikhs celebrating Diwali.

Fact

Like Hindus, many Sikhs clean their homes and places of work at Diwali. Then they light candles and lamps and celebrate with fireworks, the exchange of gifts and a feast. In Amritsar, the Golden Temple is specially lit, and its many treasures, including weapons, ancient texts and other important objects, are put on display.

> Today, it is springtime in my household. I sing Your Glorious Praises, O Infinite Lord God ... Joining with God's companions, I have begun to play. I celebrate the festival of Holi by serving the Saints.
>
> Guru Granth Sahib 1180:3–4

Hola Mohalla

The spring festival of colour **Hola Mohalla** usually happens in March. Guru Gobind Singh created a three-day Sikh festival that coincided with the Hindu festival of Holi. The name Hola Mohalla can be translated as 'military procession'. The tenth Guru used this festival as a way of training Sikh soldiers and honing their skills. It is marked in the Punjab today with military and martial arts displays.

Gurpurbs

Sikhs also hold 20 festivals every year called **Gurpurbs**. These mark the births and deaths of the Ten Gurus. Major Gurpurbs include those that remember the martyrdoms of Guru Arjan and Guru Tegh Bahadur. However, the most important Gurpurb is the one held in November, marking the anniversary of Guru Nanak's birth.

Gurpurbs are celebrated with worship at the gurdwara. This includes a full, continuous reading of the Guru Granth Sahib, which takes about 48 hours to complete. Hymns are sung in the Diwan Hall and langar is shared.

Key vocabulary

Bandi Chhor Diwas A festival where Sikhs celebrate the release of Guru Hargobind from prison

Gurpurb A festival to mark the birth or death of a Guru

Hola Mohall A Sikh adaption of the Hindu spring festival of Holi, involving military displays

Vaisakhi The Sikh festival marking the start of the new year; it also remembers the foundation of the Khalsa by Guru Gobind Singh in 1699

Sikhs celebrating a Gurpurb.

Check your understanding

1. What do Sikhs celebrate at Vaisakhi?
2. Why do Sikhs remember Guru Hargobind at Diwali?
3. Why did Guru Gobind Singh initiate the festival of Hola Mohalla?
4. How do Sikhs celebrate Gurpurbs?
5. Why do you think having festivals is important for Sikhs?

What do Sikhs believe about war?

Sikhism has a tradition of defending itself from violent threats and many Sikh soldiers have been commended for their bravery in global conflicts, but do Sikhs believe it is always right to fight?

Sikhs celebrate the festival of Hola Mohalla by displaying sword fighting and martial arts.

Since the time of the early Gurus, Sikhs have faced violent persecution. At times, this has threatened the existence of the Sikh religion. After the martyrdom of Guru Hargobind's father, Arjan, Hargobind wore two swords as a sign of Sikh power and his army won important victories against the Mughal Empire. Guru Gobind Singh developed this military tradition by establishing the Khalsa as a fighting force of people who would willingly give their lives in defence of Sikhism. He trained Sikhs in battle and made military displays a central part of the Sikh festival Hola Mohalla.

Sikh rules for fighting war

Most Sikhs believe that war should be a last resort. People should only fight to defend themselves or others who are innocent. The Guru Granth Sahib encourages people to live together peacefully: 'No one is my enemy, and no one is a stranger. I get along with everyone.' However, the Gurus were aware that this was not always possible.

In 1704, Guru Gobind Singh and the Sikhs fought a battle against the army of the Mughal Emperor Aurangzeb. The Guru was disgusted by the dishonest tactics used against the Sikhs. After escaping the battle, he wrote a letter to the emperor. This is known as the **Zafarnama**, meaning 'letter of victory', and contains the verse shown in the margin which sums up Sikh beliefs about the use of violence in war.

> 66 When all efforts to restore peace prove useless and no words avail Lawful is the flash of steel. It is right to draw the sword. 99

This teaches Sikhs that war should be a last resort. Sikh rules also state that civilians must not be deliberately harmed, no places of worship (of any faith) should be damaged, and enemy soldiers who surrender or are injured should not be harmed.

Sikhs fighting for Britain

During the First and Second World Wars the Punjab was part of the British Empire. The British were impressed by the military skill of Sikhs and so recruited them to the British army. Approximately 125,000 Sikh soldiers fought for Britain during the First World War. Most of them had never left the Punjab before, so they found the cold weather and muddy conditions particularly difficult. One Sikh soldier described his experience of battle in a letter home:

> ❝ We fix bayonets and look towards the enemy. The enemy trenches are two yards off. They have been well built. In front is barbed wire and we are not expected to attack here. With a shout to our Guru we hurl ourselves forward. The enemies bullets scorch our heroes while machine guns and cannons spread their shot upon us. ❞

Several Sikhs are listed on the Menin Gate memorial in Ypres, Belgium. The monument lists the names of thousands of soldiers from Britain and its Empire who fought in Belgium and whose bodies were never found.

A Sikh member of the Queen's Guard.

To mark the 100th anniversary of the First World War, and to recognise the sacrifices made by Sikhs during the conflict, a crowdfunding campaign raised over £22,000 to build a statue at the British National Memorial Arboretum in Staffordshire. The statue was unveiled in 2015 at a ceremony that included traditional Sikh prayers and a minute's silence.

Sikhs in the army today

There are around 150 Sikhs serving in the British army today. They include Simranjit Singh and Sarvit Singh, who in 2009 became the first Sikhs to serve in the Queen's Guard at Buckingham Palace. This made the news because they wore turbans rather than the soldiers' traditional bearskin hats. Army regulations state that the Five Ks can be worn as part of military uniform. However, when in battle, soldiers have to wear a helmet and body armour. There is ongoing research into developing bulletproof turbans.

Key vocabulary

Zafarnama A letter written by Guru Gobind Singh to the Mughal emperor; it is the basis of many Sikh beliefs about war

Check your understanding

1. What was Guru Gobind Singh's attitude to war? Refer to the Zafarnama.
2. When do Sikhs believe it is acceptable to fight?
3. Describe the experience of Sikh soldiers during the First World War.
4. How do Sikhs serve in the army today?
5. 'Sikhism is a peaceful religion.' Discuss this statement.

Unit 2: Sikhism in the modern world
Sikhism in the UK

How did Sikhism become an established religion in the UK?

There are many thousands of Sikhs living in the UK today. The majority can trace their origins back to Sikhs who emigrated from the Punjab from the 1950s onwards. Many left at this time because the splitting of the Punjab between India and Pakistan made life difficult for Sikhs. Others were simply seeking a better quality of life, work and education. Since arriving in Britain, Sikhs have made many significant contributions to British society.

The first Sikh in the UK

During the mid-nineteenth century, Sikhs in the Punjab fought a number of wars against the invading British army. Having been defeated, the Sikh ruler of the Punjab, Duleep Singh, was exiled to Britain in 1854 at the age of just 15. He lived as a British aristocrat in various castles and palaces.

Duleep Singh.

Shortly before he was brought to Britain, Duleep Singh converted to Christianity. Some say he was forced to do so. Duleep Singh died in Paris in 1893 at the age of 55. Because he had returned to Sikhism, Singh wanted to be cremated and have his ashes scattered in India, according to Sikh tradition, but he was given a Christian burial. He was only allowed to return to his homeland twice, very briefly, because the British believed that if he were to do so then Sikhs in the Punjab would again rise up against the Empire.

Gurdwaras

The first known gurdwara in Britain was built in 1911 in Putney, London. Today, there are over 250 gurdwaras in the UK, including the largest Sikh temple outside India. The Gurdwara Sri Guru Singh Sabha in Southall, London, opened in 2003. The building can hold 3000 worshippers and the langar is large enough to serve over 20,000 meals during Sikh festivals. The gurdwara also includes a library, exhibition and teaching space and in 2009 helped to open a new primary school, which is open to Sikh and non-Sikh children. At the school, Sikh and Punjabi studies are taught alongside other subjects.

The Gurdwara Sri Guru Singh Sabha in Southall, London, cost £17.5 million to build.

Controversy over interfaith marriage

In 2016, police were called to a gurdwara near Coventry. It was reported that over 50 masked men with knives had forced their way into the temple to protest against the marriage of a Sikh girl to a Hindu boy. In 2015, the **Sikh Council** had issued guidance to gurdwaras, saying that only two Sikhs should marry at a gurdwara. However, it also stated that protests should stop and that people should act in a peaceful and non-threatening manner. The police later confirmed that most of the weapons had been kirpans, one of the Five Ks worn by Khalsa Sikhs.

Traditionally, Sikhs have married within their community, but it is becoming more common for Sikhs to marry outside their faith. Some are concerned that this may lead to the religion disappearing and want to stop interfaith marriages. Others argue that the Gurus taught love, acceptance and respect for different beliefs and therefore Sikhs in the UK should be free to marry whomever they love. Some Sikhs argue that interfaith marriage is acceptable, but if a marriage takes place at a gurdwara it can only be between two Sikhs.

The future

Sikhism is a growing religion in the UK and it is often seen as having integrated successfully into British society. In particular, its focus on equality and sewa have helped promote fairness and respect for all people. Like all major religions, Sikhism faces the challenge of how to adapt to the modern world, but as it does so Sikhs remain focused on the unchanging message of the Gurus, particularly the first revelation of Guru Nanak over 500 years ago:

> 66 [There is] no Hindu nor Muslim, but only man. So whose path shall I follow? I shall follow God's path. God is neither Hindu nor Muslim and the path which I follow is God's. 99

A Sikh woman, Sim Kaur, who married a non-Sikh, describes what she sees as the real issues relating to inter-faith marriages.

> 66 Our gurdwaras are run by men and the protesters are all men. All the cancellations [of weddings] I've heard about have been of Sikh women marrying non-Sikh men or men not born into the Sikh religion and I doubt that's a coincidence. I do believe it's a faith issue, but it's also about gender and race. 99

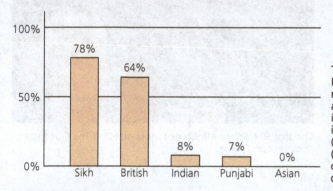

The annual British Sikh Report, which conducts research into Sikh attitudes, showed that in 2016 Sikhs in the UK identify as being 'Sikh' (78 per cent) and 'British' (64 per cent). None of the respondents self-described as 'Asian'.

Key vocabulary

Sikh Council The largest organisation representing Sikhs in the UK

Check your understanding

1. Who was the first Sikh to come to the UK?
2. Where is the largest Sikh temple outside India?
3. Why has interfaith marriage caused controversy among some Sikhs?
4. How did UK Sikhs define themselves in the 2016 annual Sikh report?
5. 'A married couple should share the same faith.' Discuss this statement, and refer to Sikhism in your answer.

Unit 2: Sikhism in the modern world
Knowledge organiser

Key vocabulary

atma The soul

Bandi Chhor Diwas A festival where Sikhs celebrate the release of Guru Hargobind from prison

chauri A fan traditionally used by rulers but now waved over the Guru Granth Sahib as a sign of respect

dhan Material sewa

Diwan Hall The main hall in a gurdwara, where worship services take place

Gurmukh Someone who puts God and the teachings of the Gurus at the centre of their life

Gurpurb A festival to mark the birth or death of a Guru

Hola Mohall A Sikh adaption of the Hindu spring festival of Holi, involving military displays

karma The forces that influence people's future rebirths

Kirtan Sohila An evening prayer that is also said during a Sikh funeral

man Mental sewa

Manmukh Someone who is self-centred and does not put God at the centre of life

Maya The temporary and illusory nature of the world

mukti Union with Waheguru; to escape the world of illusion and the cycle of life, death and rebirth

Nishan Sahib A flag that flies over every gurdwara

pilgrimage A journey taken to a place of religious importance

sarovar The pool of water that surrounds the Golden Temple

Sewa Selfless service to others

Sikh Council The largest organisation representing Sikhs in the UK

takht The throne on which the Guru Granth Sahib is placed each day for services in the gurdwara

tan Physical sewa

Vaisakhi The Sikh festival marking the start of the new year; it also remembers the foundation of the Khalsa by Guru Gobind Singh in 1699

Zafarnama A letter written by Guru Gobind Singh to the Mughal emperor; it is the basis of many Sikh beliefs about war

Key people

Jarnail Singh Bhindranwale A Sikh leader leader who with his supporters occupied the Golden Temple in 1984, demanding rights for Sikhs

Indira Gandhi An Indian Prime Minister who ordered the army to clear Sikh protesters from the Golden Temple in 1984; she was later murdered by two of her Sikh bodyguards

Mahatma Gandhi An Indian Hindu leader who campaigned for Indian independence from Britain in non-violent ways

Duleep Singh The first Sikh to live in the UK

Manmohan Singh The first Sikh Prime Minister of India

Ravinder Singh A British Sikh who founded Khalsa Aid in 1999

The first Sikh Prime Minister of India meeting The Queen at Buckingham Palace.

Key facts

- Sikhs believe that we are all in a cycle of birth, death and rebirth. We can influence our rebirth by our actions in this life (karma). Performing good deeds creates good karma; living selfishly creates bad karma.

- The ultimate goal is to achieve mukti – freedom from this cycle and union with God.

- The Sikh place of worship is called a gurdwara. An orange flag called a Nishan Sahib always flies above a gurdwara.

- During Sikh worship services, the Guru Granth Sahib is placed on a throne in the Diwan Hall; the people all sit on the floor during the service.

- The langar is a communal place for cooking and eating; every gurdwara must have a langar, which is open to everyone, whatever their gender, ethnicity or religion.

- In recent years, many non-Sikhs living in poverty have started to visit langars to have a meal each day. This has led to Sikh organisations such as SWAT taking langar on to the streets to help even more people.

- Sewa, serving others, is a key Sikh belief. There are three forms of sewa: tan (physical service), man (mental service) and dhan (material service, which includes giving to charity).

- The Harmandir Sahib, or Golden Temple, at Amritsar is the holiest place in the world for Sikhs. It receives 5.5 million visitors a year.

- The Golden Temple has been the site of two violent events in its history: the Amritsar Massacre in 1919 and Operation Blue Star in 1984.

- The Sikh festival of Vaisakhi marks the start of the new year and is also a celebration of the founding of the Khalsa.

- The festival of Bandi Chhor Diwas is on the same day as the Hindu festival of Diwali and commemorates the release of Guru Hargobind from prison.

- Gurpurbs are festivals held throughout the year to mark the births and deaths of the Ten Gurus.

- Sikhs believe it is acceptable to fight as long as this is a last resort and is in self-defence or in defence of innocent people. Rules for fighting state that civilians cannot be deliberately harmed and that no religious building – of any faith – should be damaged.

- Many Sikhs fought for Britain during the First and Second World Wars, and recently Sikhs have become members of the Queen's Guard at Buckingham Palace.

- Most Sikhs in the UK today are descendants of people who left the Punjab after the partition of India in 1949. However, there were Sikhs in the UK beforehand, and the first gurdwara was built in London in 1911.

- In recent years there has been controversy over marriages between Sikhs and people of other faiths, with some Sikhs concerned that this may lead to the extinction of the Sikh religion in the long term. Other Sikhs stress the idea of equality that Sikhism embraces and say that Sikhs should be free to marry whomever they love.

Sikhs light candles at the Golden Temple at Amritsar to celebrate the anniversary of Guru Nanak's birth.

Index

Acknowledgements

Text

p36 The Navajivan Trust for an extract by Mohandas Gandhi from *The Words of Gandhi*, 2001. Reproduced with permission from the Navajivan Trust, India; p82 The Office of His Holiness the Dalai Lama for a quotation from His Holiness the Dalai Lama, on the significance of pilgrimage for Buddhists, http://www.dalailama.com/. Reproduced with kind permission; p85 Parallax Press for 'A poem by Maha Ghosananda', reprinted from *Step by Step: Meditations on Wisdom and Compassion* (1992) by Maha Ghosananda with permission of Parallax Press, Berkeley, California, www.parallax.org; p118 Jasvir Singh BBC *Thought for the Day*, copyright © 2010–2017 City Sikhs; p127 Omissi, David, *Indian Voices of the Great War. Soldiers' letters*, 1914–18, London, 1999. With permission of Springer; p129 Sunny Hundal © The Independent, 4 October 2015, used with permission.

Photographs

Cover and title page robert stoetzel/Alamy; Chonlatip Hirunsatitporn/Shutterstock; saiko3p/Shutterstock, p7 robert stoetzel/Alamy, pp8–9 Cultura RM/Alamy Stock Photo, p10 Schita/Alamy Stock Photo, p11 l Finnian M.M. Gerety, p11 r imageBroker/Alamy Stock Photo, p12 Historical Images Archive/Alamy Stock Photo, p13 t FotoFlirt/Alamy Stock Photo, p13 b Dinodia Photos/Alamy Stock Photo, p14 t Art Directors & Trip/Alamy Stock Photo, p14 b robertharding/Alamy Stock Photo, p15 laverock/Shutterstock, p16 t Universal Images Group North America LLC/Alamy Stock Photo, p16 b Heritage Image Partnership Ltd/Alamy Stock Photo, p17 Rudra Narayan Mitra/Shutterstock, p18 t Pep Roig/Alamy Stock Photo, p18 b pimpkinpie/Alamy Stock Photo, p19 Dmitry Kalinovsky/Shutterstock, p20 t Artdirectors & Trip/Alamy Stock Photo, p20 b Zuma Press, Inc./Alamy Stock Photo, p21 Roland Pargeter/Alamy Stock Photo, p22 robertharding/Alamy Stock Photo, p23 t imageBROKER/Alamy Stock Photo, p23 b Dinodia Photos/Alamy Stock Photo, p24 t dinodia Photos/Alamy Stock Photo, p24 b commons.wikimedia.org, p25 t Godong/Alamy Stock Photo, p25 b Eric Fahmer/Shutterstock, pp28–29 Maciej Dakowicz/Alamy Stock Photo, p30 t Art Directors & Trip/Alamy Stock Photo, p30 b Tim Gainey/Alamy Stock Photo, p31 saiko3p/Shutterstock, p32 t StanislavBeloglazov/Shutterstock, p32 b tantrik71/Shutterstock, p33 theaskaman306/Shutterstock, p34 Graham Oliver/Alamy Stock Photo, p35 t Calvin Chan/Shutterstock, p35 b reddees/Shutterstock, p36 Joerg Boethling/Alamy Stock Photo, p37 t Mondadori Portfolio/Getty Images, p37 b Indranil Mukherjee/AFP/Getty Images, p38 reddees/Shutterstock, p39 Hulton Archive/Getty Images, p40 Frank Bienewald/LightRocket via Getty Images, p41 Image Source Plus/Alamy Stock Photo, p42 Tim Gainey/Alamy Stock Photo, p43 t The India Today Group/Getty Images, p43 b STRDEL/AFP/Getty Images, p44 Photos 12/Alamy Stock Photo, p45 t Pacific Press/Alamy Stock Photo, p45 b K. Decha/Shutterstock, p47 t Dinodia Photos/Alamy Stock Photo, p47 b neelsky/Shutterstock, p49 Chonlatip Hirunsatitporn/Shutterstock, pp50–51 happydancing/Shutterstock, p52 Nila Newsom/Shutterstock, p54 t Godong/Universal Images Group via Getty Images, p54 b Kittiwongsakul/AFP/Getty Images, p55 British Library/Robana/REX/Shutterstock, p56 t Godong/Alamy Stock Photo, p56 b Granger Historical Picture Archive/Alamy Stock Photo, p57 REX/Shutterstock, p58 Ernst Christen/Shutterstock, p59 Ivy Close Images/Alamy Stock Photo, p60 Yaacov Shein/Alamy Stock Photo, p61 t Pascal Deloche/Getty Images, p61 b TongFotoman/Shutterstock, p62 wikipedia.org, p63 t Albachiaraa/Shutterstock, p63 b weniliou/Shutterstock, p64 James Barr/Alamy Stock Photo, p64 b John Brown/Alamy Stock Photo, p65 Man of the Mountain/Shutterstock, p66 commons.wikimedia.org, p67 Chirawan Thaiprasansap/Shutterstock, p69 Hemis/Alamy Stock Photo, pp70–71 Man of the Mountain/Shutterstock, p72 canan kaya/Shutterstock, p73 defpicture/Shutterstock, p75 t robertharding/Alamy, p75 b Nadezda Murmakova/Shutterstock, p76 Vasin Lee/Shutterstock, p77 t Steve Heap/Shutterstock, p77 b John Brown/Alamy Stock Photo,